CORPORATE MERGERS
TRANSITIONING THE
AMERICAN ECONOMY

CORPORATE MERGERS TRANSITIONING THE AMERICAN ECONOMY

Corporate Buyouts and a Junk Bond
Market Out of Control

JAYSON REEVES

and
The Hurn Foundation

iUniverse, Inc.
Bloomington

Corporate Mergers Transitioning the American Economy
Corporate Buyouts And A Junk Bond Market Out Of Control

iUniverse books may be ordered through booksellers or by contacting:

iUniverse
1663 Liberty Drive
Bloomington, IN 47403
www.iuniverse.com
1-800-Authors (1-800-288-4677)

ISBN: 978-1-4759-3783-1 (sc)
ISBN: 978-1-4759-3784-8 (e)
ISBN: 978-1-4759-3785-5 (dj)

Library of Congress Control Number: 2012912457

Printed in the United States of America

iUniverse rev. date: 10/15/2012

INTRODUCTION

|||||||||||||||||||||||||||||||||||||||||||||||||||||||||

Observing how the American economy before and after the year 2000 has been transitioned by corporate mergers, and junk bond issues, the American society of people, businesses, and government has had to change with the times, and overcome various diversified issues. Some corporate mergers or buyouts have affected the U.S. economy in ways that consisted of conflicting losses of tax revenue for government, and then businesses struggling to reorganize or survive. These have been major factors throughout corporate merger and buyout acquisitions regulated by government, but also some financial transactions have consisted of executive greed, fraud, and certain issues that are not consistent with certain laws, and the U.S. Constitution. Considering these facts some corporate mergers or buyouts with certain executives are good for a vast amount of people, and issues in America if they are transitioned in a productive way of restructuring with new, or productive management.

The American business transaction and process of a corporate merger or takeover issue can be observed within the good, and bad of various corporate, or government business concerns. These are transactions with the U.S. economy becoming an assortment of conflicts or business restructuring. The corporate takeover and buyout issues within the American society are also part of the business observation, and conditions of law that occasionally have needs to be reviewed. This is logical to management values for long term U.S. economic, and social disciplines of prosperity. Understanding this, for hundreds of years people have bought, sold, and or restructured these businesses similar to any other type of agreement within real property, and this has an economic effect, and repercussion. Contrary to these facts, this is valid with the U.S. amended laws, tax revenue, and profitable earnings that keep the

American society of governed assets productive which is not a new challenge.

The Securities & Exchange Commission (SEC) is a big part of this process with regulation, but their U.S. government activity in these markets are perceptional only sense the 1930s, and more so for publicly traded company issues. Even the chairmanship turnover rate has been somewhat intense (c/o needing to improve lawful enforcement) from 1990 with Richard Breeden, then Harvey Pitt, Christopher Cox, and now in 2012 Mary Shapiro as U.S. SEC regulators. This is the observation that some financial crimes were not considered with enforcement good enough. Upon most relevant disciplines the SEC with some state and federal legislative matters also included these subjects corrected by judicial government procedures. These judicial concerns have been the increasing awareness of government regulation, and some enforcement that seemed occasionally too late to save some peoples investments, and or retirement savings of "money".

These factors of government become relevant conditions of business laws, financial market laws, and laws governing technology. This is understood from the overall tremendously changing times, and decades of business in America, and some worldwide concerns. Observing this, the past decades and centuries have consisted of the expansion of diversified markets with logical tax revenue for government to function. This is important throughout America with some U.S. investors earning occasional, and or appropriate financial benefits, but more so with government having additional money to operate.

Another review of business will also outline how various issues within corporate mergers, takeovers, and buyouts in America have changed regional business matters of the economy. This includes the fact that some local governments within cities, and towns have ran tremendously low on money to operate when a large corporation restructures, and or relocates certain divisions of business from their region. These connected resources of business are also a financial leveraging process that is part of a "junk bond" market that was slightly out of control, contrary to the duties of the SEC regulators.

This includes trillions of dollars occasionally in limbo somewhere conditionally observed by the United States government, or in a foreign country restrained by issues of international law. Considering these factors some issues even apply to the U.S. National Debt especially if you recognize Ameritech Corporation, WorldCom Corporation, Enron Corporation, and a vast amount of others with domestic, and more so foreign business dealings.

The individual states, and the United States federal government has had to endure the opportunities of economic gains, and losses of various corporate mergers, and even hostile corporate takeovers by virtue of certain social values. Business and social values such as WorldCom, Enron, and a few others have been disastrous for American people as investors in certain business issues causing critical problems to their financial disciplines of employment, or a business operation. These are vitally important issues that apply to business in America with short, and long term investment decisions, but they should have consisted of more lawful security.

A vast amount of corporate American transactions also apply to good, and bad foreign relations. Some of these matters include U.S. National Security concerns due to large corporate assets of vital defense, and security interest who's losses became a vital need of "business, and social restructuring". This even applies to the prosperity of American corporations like Zenith Corporation, ConocoPhillips Corporation, ExxonMobil Corporation, and BP-Amoco Oil Corporation (c/o now BP of America & London) that has lacked some business liability concerns. Then this includes various buyout purchases by General Electric Corporation during the tenure of Jack Welch, their former CEO which has held some good issues of liability.

Another corporate buyout of conflict consist of certain events surrounding the R.J. Reynolds Tobacco Company which became another massive corporate issue within future business concerns of existence. The R.J. Reynolds Tobacco Company is an American established business that won't easily be the same as they once were. This has been factual for the last 2 decades after they were bought-out by "Kohlberg Kravis Roberts & Company " (KKR) an investment banking company. The logic of this transaction consisted of the R.J. Reynolds Tobacco Company which was purchased for $25 billion dollars by KKR in 1987. The economic format of this transaction also included the R.J. Reynolds Tobacco Company's issues within debt to close the deal. Their business holdings also included their subsidiary of RJR Nabisco which means that R.J. Reynolds Tobacco Co held a large part of the American market of snack food items, and tobacco products. Therefore the transition of the largest corporation's with various commodities throughout America serve various concerns for the people, government, and the American society of business with progressive disciplines.

Observing other factual issues of corporate activity included the buyout transactions of Inland Steel Corporation, LTV Steel Corporation, and Bethlehem Steel Corporation. These where corporate issues purchased by Wilber Ross an American (c/o International Steel Group), and then the ArcelorMittal Steel "Group" (c/o Lakshmi Mittal) from India with certain European invested interest. Within the logic that most of these corporations were U.S. Defense contractors, it also included Zenith Corporation being bought out by LG Electronics which is a South Korean company with some U.S Defense technology concerns. Most of these corporate mergers, and various hostile corporate takeover issues were part of a vicious "junk-bond" market in America throughout the decades of the 1980s, and 1990s. Upon these transitional merger/buyout conditions other activity in the past years consisted of the "Corporate Raider Concerns" applied by additional people like T-Boone Pickens, Ted Turner, Robert Johnson, Carl Icahn, Frank Lorenzo, and a few others. These Corporate American Raiders, and other U.S. investors may have been more productive than foreign investors buying U.S. companies contrary to argumentative greenmail factors!

These issues of publicly held corporations, the U.S. Securities & Exchange Commission, and the American system of government have been the pivotal factor of discipline within these corporate takeover transactions. The pivotal factor now deems to consist of the global economic, and the business concept of issues that have invaded America with good, and sometimes more so bad foreign related products, and issues of concern. Considering this combination of issues upon which also applies to U.S. Anti-Trust laws, and the laws of the United States Constitution, these are the values of government tax revenue, business revenue, and the good and bad challenges of business survival or expansion in America.

Small businesses which have potential to expand also have a need to grow without illegal business competitive conflicts which may include buying into another company or business to be part of this revenue, and economic transitional process. These issues of business decisions to expand by way, and virtue of mergers, buyouts, or takeovers also has other concerns which becomes the logic within the rate of employment for the American people. The people of America have observed these conflicts in many different ways, but these changing times are similar to the Great Depression observing a 70 year difference when vital laws are ignored as it applies to technology, and sociology. Then small, and large transitioning businesses have lawful opportunities from values within U.S. Anti-Trust laws, and most human, and lawful rights of the U.S. Constitution which on too many occasions have been ignored causing other harmful effects.

The transition of the American economy had potential to be better, but with a vast amount of legal, and business issues, "Corporate American and small business failures" occurred. These are conflicting values upon which have been a large part of losses within government tax revenue. Losses of tax revenue for the American society are also causing a tremendous level of challenge's for government to expand or have a surplus. Also these become the challenges that the American system of government will have to evaluate thru budget governed disciplines. This evaluation will have to be conducted or pursued with discipline in the near future, "before" the future U.S. economy is inside-out. The logic of this includes "foreign businesses or government" (c/o China, Japan, or others) controlling a majority of the United States currency. These are conditional conflicts which are "only" slightly hypothetical of "Third World" countries compared to America. Upon this logic of evaluation these are more so considered poor people in other countries with a stronger money circulation that are manufacturing products cheaper than they are made, and cost in America. Therefore some American businesses are failing with foreign issues of currency gaining control of the American dollar, and this makes the dollar weaker in the United States.

What various currency valued issues are actually doing is that the combination of countries like India, Japan, China, and others (c/o even parts of Europe) in the next 25 to 35 years could have currency that can possibly be worth more than the American dollar. That could be imagining paying *5.00 dollars to *1.00 yen, and the U.S. National Deficit at over $5, $10, or even $20 trillion dollars. Sadly this also may be a compared conflict of the United States being attacked by a foreign enemy nation with multiple nuclear guided missiles, or destructive terrorist attacks. More so the amount of American's that are victimized by severe floods, tornados, hurricanes, and other natural disasters has also set back hundreds of thousands of Americans. Then even more so these problems can increase if America becomes weaker, and then cannot rebuild similar to some other developed nations, or even developing third world countries.

The American National Debt, and the Gross National Product in competition with Japan, China, Korea, Mexico, and one or two other nations is two conditional "national indicators" of valid concern. These indicators apply to products that people with businesses manufacture, and sale to a variety of consumers (c/o a money circulation) in various countries. This indicator of discipline is based on sales, and the manufacturing of product issues. Even more so lately this has become the observed loss of United States manufacturing resources with sales, tax revenue, and employment issues.

Debt, and the Gross National Product within American values have taken on tremendous pressure from other countries with responsible business, and foreign control of formerly American owned companies. Contrary to these factors of conflicting transitions, most social values in these governed societies consist of nations with diverse establishments of a government, or even a parliament. This also applies to U.S. National Security, and the true value of global, and more so American business owners which becomes an endless value. These valued issues then become the part of other conflicts or valued issues of social, economic, management, and labor issues of indifference. Therefore businesses are a factual part of the transition as it applies to the mergers, takeovers, buyouts, or developing businesses that structure a nation's economy.

Most American subjects of capitalism is concurred when observing certain corporations whom try to survive the true value within corporate merger restructuring. This includes whether the restructuring is helpful within the need of business progress or a requirement of government applicable to tax revenue or not. Contrary to these factors this is more so the other productive issues of business that helps investors, and society with progressive prosperity. Upon this logic, corporations that are restructured apart from failing to do productive business becomes a valuable issue from the small, and large businesses affecting the U.S. economy.

Foreign business issues with corporate products that are manufactured with lower labor cost, and sometimes low material cost occasionally give American business competitors a slightly harder time in their own nation-wide market. To some vital extent of liability within government this includes the American system of the courts, and various Justice Department concerns if various product specifications or certain laws are not considered. Therefore our American values of capitalism become conflicting, and somewhat must be appealed or supported by the lawful value applied to the U.S. Constitution, and laws that allow business, and the people to prosper with domestic tranquility.

Capitalism with gains and losses is applied, and recognized within the number of transactions that occurred with businesses such as British Petroleum (c/o Amoco), and just as well the Exxon Corporation (before ExxonMobil) whom suffered expensive disasters. These expensive accidents at Amoco, and Exxon caused problems affecting their future economic concerns, not to mention some parts of the environment. The logic of these companies have tried to restructure differently apart from the problems of corporations such as WorldCom, and Enron with their corporate concept of manipulated-fraud, and greed. Contrary to corporate fraud we have found, and observed a reduction of true capitalist when positive business efforts are reduced with unlawful production or manipulation. This has been applied from positive corporate constituents such as ConocoPhillips Corporation, and now the merger of Continental Airlines Incorporated, and United Airlines Corporation (as United Continental Holding Inc.) which now is 2 businesses instead of 4. Then America has taken a loss with the remaining format of American business reductions that also support the people.

Considering various U.S. airlines, and oil companies operate worldwide with additional national security, the U.S. government, and most businesses have a duty to occasionally work together. This becomes an issue within observation of the American system of government supporting citizens, and corporate business values. Also a vast amount of these companies were diversely affected by the September 11, 2001 terrorist attacks causing part of this fading amount of corporate business constituents. A fading amount of tax revenue and employment generating losses in corporate, and business operations means that the former employees will have to restructure their economic future within planning. This resource of problems also factored a loss of revenue earnings, people within being occasional employees with job security, and various business assets, or products to sometimes suffer.

Observing issues in 2001 the American Airlines Corporation's merger with Trans World Airlines (TWA) had a reduction effect to the amount of corporate businesses in America. This becomes an important evaluation concerning the amount of opportunities that businesses in their logical operational existence will maintain, and the logic that they will provide to ambitious American's. This was applied to a growing conflict of business, and therefore America has been compiling a loss similar to the conditions of a third world country. This equation is valued with a losing structure of taxable business revenue, and opportunities of capitalism to survive in business. Upon this becoming a crisis, the Troubled Asset Relief Program (TARP) was established by the U.S. federal government.

This became the concern which made government involvement in the TARP liquidity restructuring of certain banks, and businesses critical. Then contrary to TARP funding or other economic crisis concerns, the restructuring of various professions with a lack of U.S. Constitutional efficiency have caused a destructive set back to a developing nation such as America that must be corrected.

As we observe massive business values, most merger/buyout transition concerns are considered with various corporate disciplines. These transactions are also recognized within some complacent conflicts of government which are legal disciplines of order thru the courts, the legislature, and various productive people. Considering this, if the courts and the judiciary do their job to the best of their ability, its strongly possible the executive, and legislative branches of American government may understand a better logic of more people, and businesses to expand. This becomes the major element with the American transition of small, large, expandable or well established corporations of America that keeps society prosperous, and having expanded resources. With various laws being ignored this has affected small expanding businesses, responsible government for the people, and or the businesspeople that could have made a better difference other than greed, or self-indulgence. These issues also may default; therefore they become the important subjects for workable components from smaller, or larger corporate business issues in America to survive, and prosper without unlawful conflict.

Throughout America, if people, and major business survival consist of not just transitioning a move to Mexico, or other countries with a low governed currency system like India, Africa, and Indonesia this transition becomes the root of various challenge's. The Whirlpool Corporation buyout of Maytag Corporation, and other major appliance manufactures have exceeded logical U.S. Constitutional compromise (c/o foreign interest), but this American business has strong market, and business reservations of Canada, and the Canadian government. Observing this logic, and certain market issues, the Whirlpool Corporation expanding to Mexico has meant that this American business has slightly given up on the American workforce, but with business expansion issues worldwide. These are the societal, and government disciplines that are questionable to keep logical levels of prosperity, and domestic tranquility in a livable, and sustainable economic order. These are concerned issues that affect all types of American regions, but American management, and labor fair competitive values will be the logic from this conflict of global expansion. Then the U.S. logic of prosperity will require good, and not bad or destructive foreign relations.

Most major American oil company's operate in 3rd world countries or low currency rate income countries whom have dictators as government officials. Lately these are countries near the Middle East, and Africa that consist of conflicting foreign relations compared to America, and it's Constitutional values which require legal observation, and enforcement concerns when certain issues must be kept in order. These "internationally" competitive levels of concern also include inflation, and various natural resources throughout other countries. Then these business, and social issues are sometimes part of unreliable labor standards that have become factual to maintain a safe society of industrial processes.

Understanding these concerns during the 1990s, and the first decade of 2000 American industry suffered from a ration of accidents, or high levels of financial fraud, and complacent conflicts of danger. Some of these issues of danger consisted of industrial processes with fatal explosions, negligence, and even issues of terrorism. Considering this, American industry standards with liability all of a sudden were experiencing the same types of accidents that certain foreign countries (c/o Asia, South America, and others) consist of with "bad" communist dictatorship issues of government. Then understanding this, most international, and U.S. domestic businesses have had some conditional suffering within establishing arbitrational industry values. These were factual problems which applies to these industry sectored businesses, and their front line within observed economic stability of existence.

When certain large corporations, and some small businesses have resource's within future survival, some of their next decisions consist of solid investment concerns, and more so corporate mergers with businesses that could boost their future stability, and economic earnings. Considering these factual issues, all large American corporations, and small expanding businesses must be astute in their format of liabilities, any possible international relations, and their managing of business liquidity. Most valuable government (c/o the U.S.A.) issues of discipline then play an important role between the people, and all types of business. This then equates "business, and government liquidity" revenue which conditionally applies to our U.S. Constitutional values of manageable prosperity disciplines to compromise future resources, and domestic tranquility.

Understanding various workable standards with compromising concerns valued for business, certain people ignored some vital conditions of national security "extensively" causing American businesses, and people to suffer. These conditional problems that were ignored before America suffered from issues such as international investments that occasionally included international terror was the liability of various businesses, and more so government. Crime similar to treason have also been part of this equation that affected the economy, and the social values of America. The September 11, 2001 terrorist attacks which included foreign, and or some U.S. domestic conditions of people with derogatory conflicts was only one out of many vital examples.

The most severe issues of liability, and factors of compromise in expanding industries throughout America at this time are internet companies, wireless communication companies, financial brokers, and defense contractors. These and other arbitrary industry concerns consist of liability values, and an observation of the U.S. Constitutional laws that are in need of enforcement. This then becomes the format of business restructuring, or the logic of how they are restructuring from an older process within disciplines of industry. Therefore these are then valued business concerns with advanced changes in the American society.

Various liabilities are within the subject of financial fraud, and public safety with security issued business matters that America has worked to establish. These issues have become important to keep awareness throughout all industry concerns. Even as the American airline transportation industry during 2010 restructures of illegal immigration (c/o Arizona, California, & other states) which includes issues such as the recent mortgage crisis. Therefore, these issues like so many other regions in America with good, and bad neighborly state government, and corporate business concerns is part of what can cause a severe effect on an American region's economy.

Upon these factors of an economy from industry values, a person can observe the issues of bankruptcy restructuring through corporate mergers or buyouts as an issue that has caused a future of severe caution within most good, and bad financial, and social conditions. These are corporate issues apart from the U.S. government consisting of levels of caution. The past years between 1990 to 2010 have consisted of corporate and business purchases that have created a logic within caution. These values of caution appropriately consist of a vast amount of colored flashing lights over terrorist concerns which applies to domestic and international alerts. These matters that include international investments, and international terror are still issues that require government committee hearings, and conflicts to be settled mostly in the courts. Some of these issues have existed with helpful protection for "Corporate American" assets when other corporations in the United States are purchased by other larger corporations, and the value of a corporate raider with logical business. Therefore this eases the tremendous losses, and control of some of the dissolution that has caused suffering to the people that are more so involved in business. These are factors in our American economy, and society that have caused a factual economic breakdown that America has considered as a recession during the years of 2008 thru 2012 that must be observed.

CONTENTS

CHAPTER ONE
CORPORATE BUYOUTS IN A JUNK BOND MARKET OUT OF CONTROL

||||||||||||||||||||||||||||||||||||||||||||||||||||||||||||||||||||||||||

Observing the American economy, and most all businesses for over 100 years, or more so the people whom have started, owned, and operated businesses they have made diversified purchases or agreements of the sale of certain corporations or businesses. This included business or corporate buying transactions that affect other business issues, government, employment, and more so the people. These issues have certain repercussion values that have applied, and appropriated conditional effects on various parts of the American society, and its economy. Upon these concerns a level of capitalism with financing or investing money upon which people, and or employers earn, inherit, or even how they exist in peoples possession is part of a process of what someone or a corporation needs or has as their ambition of prosperity. This becomes the occasional understanding of expanding a business with logical liquidity growth that is part of their plans to survive in the American format of business.

Government along with public or private business have spent decades with arguments, and discussions about what is workable, and non-workable. These argumentative factors consist of values within this process of a merger, buyout, or the takeover acquisition

1

of a business with diversified levels and procedures to reorganize. Therefore the business may have new people, and ideas which also applies to the United States Constitutional establishment of laws. This also occasionally can affect the advancements of small expanding business including even various corporate businesses with diversified products, and divisions.

During the turn of the century, and the years following 1900 that consisted of diversified businesses and various corporations which were becoming active in an environment of stock, and bond market trading, corporate America observed issues of growth with discipline. These were businesses like U.S. Steel Corporation, RCA Corporation, Eli Lilly & Company, Pfizer Inc., and Chase Bank Company. Others included a vast of "Railroad Companies" like Northfork Southern Corporation, CSX Corporation, and Union Pacific Corporation. Then Department Store's such as Sears & Robuck Company, Carson Pirie Scott & Company, Montgomery Ward's, J.C. Penney Company Inc., and now the expanding Walmart Incorporated chain of stores have achieved productive results in business for decades. These business levels of progress have resources with their discipline of why most of these businesses still have existence, and prosper with values in today's U.S. economy.

The American automobile industry within General Motors Corporation, Ford Motor Company, and Chrysler Corporation have been around sense 1910. Managing, or governing these businesses, and the people with the establishing of the financial markets is part of the investments of owning a percentage of a company which becomes complex with government, and societal issues of concern. Contrary to these factors the products, or services that can be provided are the intellectual value for most consumers, and issues of business prosperity. This also importantly becomes the consideration of what the American society has conditioned as its level of acceptable disciplines of business. Therefore this is the observation that even applies to the important issues of professionalism over the decades following the 1929 depression.

During the early 1900s the New York Stock Exchange was just becoming an active stock ownership trading market along with a vast amount of diversified businesses throughout the United States starting to compile a transition of junk bond related business issues. Other issues of market trading goes back as far as the 1700s. These become disciplines within revenue earnings, the sharing of revenue with investors, valuable products, various markets, and production facilities that most times gross enormous amounts of money. They also have provided government tax revenue which helped stimulate the American economy. Also this consist of products, and service issues that various people may consider good, and or bad for themselves, business, or even government. Even more so sometimes these service disciplines will help a smaller business expand with values that are important. Then most corporations or even small businesses can be workable with additional asset liquidity, and equity. This equity upon business progress occasionally turns junk bond values of a business into a more manageable, and productive resource of business operating disciplines. Upon these facts within considered business decisions this is valuable to the American society, the economy, and the people.

The corporate issues of junk bonds with corporate mergers was deferred with conflict for decades after the Great Depression. These became the values of what a business is worth (c/o investment ratings) to one or more individuals, or corporations which became applicable to the American system of government regulation. Apart from 1890 to the 1920s, and then during the mid-1980s this also became a market for "Corporate Raiders" such as T-Boone Pickens, Carl Icahn, Reginald Lewis, Frank Lorenzo, and brokerage firms such as Kohlberg Kravis Roberts & Company. Most of these people have been involved in extensive business issues such as corporate hostile take-over concerns. These corporate hostile takeovers, and various corporate raiders consist of good, and bad issues that determine America's corporate future which includes various employees, and people. With speculation of future business survival these financial acquisitions severely became the concerned importance of business restructuring which was less evident with only a few corporations that were restructured into productive businesses. These became the corporate business market purchase issues for ownership throughout a "conditionally vicious" junk bond market.

Upon these values between brokerage firms, investors, and corporate businesses inflation has been a prediction of conditional junk bond valued issues with economic repercussions. These values of inflation went from $10 billion dollars (c/o the 1920s) in market industry value to around $186 billion dollars during the 1980s, and 1990s. This market level of issues, and values within the use of assets, or to except conflicts that enter-phase with greed, or quality investment grade values of a corporation were sometimes useful. Some of these useful values help the American money circulation for small investors (contrary to greenmail), and the ability to expand from other business resources other than their own. Considering these factors of good, or bad opinions, and economic evaluations the course of business, and inflation will, or must continue to advance with most all good, and even bad business agreements.

Understanding the 1980s with a vicious junk bond market it also included people like Ivan Boasky, and Michael Milken whom took "illegal" insider trading to levels of financial, and economic ration. Also a junk bond resource of people with a purpose as corporate raiders was Carl Icahn the founder of Icahn & Company, Reginald Lewis the former Chairman of Beatrice International, Jack Welch the former CEO of General Electric Corporation, and T-Boone Pickens the founder of Mesa Petroleum, and BP Capital. This new $180 billion dollar plus junk bond market issue applies conflicting disciplines within the true values of various corporate acquisitions. These acquisitions consist of two (2) or an occasional other bidder as companies, and or corporate raiders involved themselves in various junk bond "projects" as of the purchasing entity, or a company. These companies, and bidder's within the business acquisition process have procedures, and more so obligations within various business ideas to be workable with future earnings. Contrary to this fact conditionally the success of a newly purchased business or corporation is not always guaranteed, but with better management some of these failing corporations are less likely to be junk bond rated businesses. These are businesses that are restructured with the understanding that there is possible, and useful prosperity with the newly established business.

Another vital observation throughout the American junk bond markets is the disciplines of law by high wage earning professionals. This became the unlawful, and different conditions from Michael Milken with his former brokerage firm of Drexel Burnham Lambert Company whom exceeded logical business resources. His duties, and activities were applied to underwriting corporate merger projects with buying the stock for clients before the corporate buyout was finalized. Ivan Boasky also heavily dealt in junk bond issues, but as financial businesspeople working in these financial markets acquire bad habits unlawfully, this is when the government has probable cause to intervene.

Between the business dealings of Michael Milken, Ivan Boasky and a few other ambitious financial executives managing merger/buyout issues, and other financial services, their duties consisted of the process of raising millions, and billions of dollars for their clients. These where vital business matters upon which Drexel Burnham Lambert Co. paid Milken commissions in excess of more than $500 million dollars before which he allegedly was prosecuted for the greed of insider trading. This legal issue outlined that he provided confidential information in a vast amount of illegal insider trading transactions before the buyout was appropriate to be public notice. These factors made various trades a resource of violations against the negotiated price agreements of the outstanding shares of stock that various companies control.

This issue of Michael Milken with insider trading is considered a problem that manipulated, and dissolved business earning's, and or purchase agreements from corporations that were a working level of sacrifice. These economic issues occurred during their occasional tuff times with various professional disciplines, and even the resource to restructure a business. A few of Michael Milken's clients consisted of the Executive Life Insurance Company, and Columbia Savings & Loan suffering losses after his level of success over the years at Drexel Burnham Lambert. Also his business dealings within transactions included a few business names such as MCI Communication;

gaining a billion dollars (c/o later none as MCI WorldCom), and even activity at Turner Broadcasting. Observation of this becomes the conditional concerns of resource within corporate buyout issues which most "hostile corporate takeovers", and other lawful acquisitions exceeding logical transfers of corporate business control hold relevant to shareholder value. This process to control another business or corporation (c/o junk bond ratings) had not existed heavily for at least five decades which more so consisted of various inflated bid, and offering price agreements. Considering this logical process, certain values include the corporation's outstanding shares which is, and can be an outside investment issue apart from employee stock ownership conditions.

Throughout 1920 to 1970, and then during the 1980s being indifferent from 50 to 80 years within the history of stock market junk bond issues of publicly traded companies, this junk bond market expanded extensively. The junk bond market of the early 1990s consisted of slower, but rational concerns of critical corporations being bought out and fewer, or at least a smaller rate of high-yield bond trading investments with value. Most of these buyouts, or purchases of businesses was slightly logical, and occasionally aggressive as they sometimes consist of unwanted businesses, or equipment assets that were valued by others. This included other issues like the recessions, and near depression concerns over the proceedings 60 years which the concept of a junk bond market went from $10 billion to over $185 billion dollars (c/o the 1980s) in market valued issues. Along with this deferred timeframe other social issues like war, and large effective Supreme Court, and Federal Court cases that the United States was enduring consisted of law case disciplines, and indirectly became a resource for a more lawfully developed society. Therefore in some concerns the American society, and the U.S. economy was applied with value to most markets as it was becoming a factor with evidence of conditional progress.

The transitioning of the American economy sense the 1980s has been a repetition of improved technology, and a variation of established laws that were occasionally ignored. With a resource of technology advancements, ignoring various U.S. Anti-Trust laws, and

U.S. Banking laws the U.S. Economy has been a critical problem as it applies to lawfully business minded Americans. This includes laws such as the Glass Steagall Act (c/o a repeal), and the Bank Holding Act of 1956 that has been part of industry that occasionally has taken some American regions full speed backwards. Another valid concern has consisted of the disciplines within the last five U.S. Presidents within Ronald Reagan, George Bush Sr., Bill Clinton, the 2nd George Bush Jr., and presently Barack Obama whom must endure depressed economic issues of arbitration. This was the arbitrary effort within various corporations seeking answers, and solutions from foreign and some domestic relief in many ways. Considering some of these solutions were an issue of overhead cost, and logical government regulation, the issue of business restructuring went in the direction of junk bond market values to increase liquidity, or asset holdings. Manipulation of assets (c/o an Endless Loop crisis) within U.S. Constitutional issues of law reached a highly destructive point with U.S. Anti-Trust laws has kept American small businesses from logical expansion just like some violent crimes. Therefore a variation of state and federal Attorney General's along with some lawyers have "not" helped or recognized certain business legal matters good enough!

Within logical factors the transition with U.S. Anti-Trust laws consisted of new Middle Eastern businesses of people doing things during the 1990s thru the 2000s that Standard Oil Company (c/o Amoco Oil), and other oil companies were outlined by law "not" to do in 1913. The anti-trust case, and legislature from government said that the Standard Oil Company including John D. Rockefeller, and all other oil companies could "not" own gas stations directly across the street from each other. In a vast amount of regions in the U.S. this has been done ether as a corporate owned business, or more so in a format of becoming independent business operates whom are mostly Middle Eastern nationalized citizen business owners. This would eliminate the unlawful control of the same oil company ownership as a city/town street corner monopoly which would extensively exclude other oil & gas business competitors.

Another factor of concern was the issues within problems of when U.S. Treasury Security Robert Ruban, President Bill Clinton, and the

U.S. Congress deregulated banking with legislature that repealed the Glass Steagall Act. This conflicting issue has seem to push the U.S. society, and the banking industry full speed backwards. Therefore these guided U.S. economic matters by government and a few other issues have become an "investment banking industry concern" which consisted of greed, conflict, and crime, not an equation of careful economic planning. These issues exceeded the normal values of investing, and the progress of small American business owners from achieving logical, and good progress. Then these efforts of expanding their business operation which sadly included the loss of $11 trillion dollars of U.S. household wealth when a bank lending crisis occurred in the first decade of 2000 became a new problem of severe concern.

Contrary to issues within competitive conflicts, various business issues have been found in American small business owners being pushed out by foreign business conflicts (c/o new citizenship issues), and a ration of financial bankers whom wanted to cater to investors at certain local, or commerce banks. This was done at certain NDB banks, Tech Federal Savings institutions, and a few others which can be a violation or challenged conflict of "repealing" the Glass Steagall Act. This was the observation of a bank wanting to increase competitive conflicts of liquidity, and industry economic opportunities. Also this included the ambition of other small investors like newly found steel workers involved in complex investments that harmed their retirements. Therefore the conflict within these values also had the considered ambition to increase their own liquidity with high-risk market equity, and stock acquisition investments even at local banks which become quite risky.

Monopolies similar to Standard Oil Corporation (c/o 1910) which even today includes the Microsoft Corporation are a concern to the United States government on occasions. This is due to intense law case arguments that outline U.S. Anti-Trust legal disciplines which did include various other laws, and regulatory conditions. Bill Gates has earned over a billion dollars of his own personal wealth from Microsoft Corp with other executives, and people close to him, and his family investing in his established company within Microsoft.

This has given the Microsoft Corporation it's strong financial value of security, and how others (apply to Standard & Poor's or Moody) rating as a publicly held company, and their business achievements, investment quality, or state of business operating condition.

Observing diversified companies that are not "Junk Bond Rated" their state of condition has tremendous values that must be managed. This factor of management issues consist of conditions of when they are occasionally too valuable or vulnerable as a private business to be bought out by other corporations, or even individual corporate raiders. Contrary to these facts during 1998 British Petroleum Company; "the largest oil company in England" completed an acquisition buyout of Amoco Oil Corporation which was formerly the Standard Oil Corporation. Between the two international issues of government within concern of London (c/o the United Kingdom), and the United States this was an American corporate buyout of relevant concern. Then understanding this buyout being one of the largest American business losses transcended on American soil going back 88 years, a tremendous level of concerns had to be considered. Amoco Oil Corporation becoming BP meant that the American society, and certain economic factors were about to become a factor in American business that has not existed for more than 5 decades. Considering this fact, this was around the same time when Japan started flooding the American markets with various products.

The value within monopolies also even more so at various times consisted of the concern that Standard Oil Corporation, and various other businesses was an important United States Department of Defense contractor. The productive business of Microsoft Corporation, and it's founder Bill Gates consist of a monopoly on the Disk Operating System (DOS) products which is considered an IBM compatibility valued computer product, and patent. Considering this, Microsoft Corporation has been carefully productive enough with manufacturing domestically, and internationally including research not to extensively need the purchase of certain other corporations to expand, but they did make investments like MSNBC. Upon comparing Microsoft Corporation, and the America Online Corporate (AOL) that were different from

pursued large investments in various corporation's to control board seats or a percentage of the company. He has also made occasional profits from the sale of certain small interesting corporate businesses offering or giving his argumentative factors of economic values which are board member, and occasionally shareholder engagement rights. These are activities within business transactions where equity investors with large investment dollar capabilities have established board of director control which may include profits within the sale of a smaller corporation with value. This was evident within Carl Icahn having investments with Bristol-Myers Squibb, and their sale of Imclone Inc. to Eli Lilly & Company. Imclone Systems Incorporated is a company that makes pharmaceutical products for diseases such as certain forms of cancer. Upon the activity of Imclone managing cancer research, the company's assets became valuable and attractive to other businesses, and the company found its self being sold to Eli Lilly & Company in 2008 for $6.5 billion dollars or $62.00 a share. This is where a large company can expand its product base with additional business resources.

The company Imclone Systems Inc. traded on the NASDAQ market with various well known investors and business owners like Martha Stewart. The conditional business success of Martha Stewart is one value, but then she violated the federal law when she sold over $200,000.00 worth of Imclone's stock as she was part of the fiduciary of the company. Her trade (c/o being prosecuted) was made on December 27, 2002 which was a day before the Food & Drug Administration (FDA) did not approve their medication Erbitux. Even the founder of Imclone Systems Inc. Samuel D. Waksal whom traded off his shares on the 27th of December 2002 was prosecuted for his sale of the stock. In addition he provided acknowledgement to friends, and family to do the same, "which they did", and this was considered insider information of confidentiality from a fiduciary to earn an "unlawful" profit. This was well over $20 million dollar's-worth of stock which was a deceptive practice of securities fraud including inside trading as it applies to option and stock trading.

Another business that endured a long-term resource of business was the Bristol-Myers Squibb Co. which was founded in 1887 upon considering they were reestablished or upgraded from a merger in 1989. The 1989 merger consisted of Bristol-Myers, and the Squibb Corporation which did not expand a business but made them stronger in terms of working together. They are 2 of a vast amount of American corporation's that merged to become stronger against even foreign, and other American pharmaceutical business conflicts. This becomes a similar corporate level of value within century old companies with logical existence that have similar values to the Eli Lilly & Company business discipline sense the 1876 establishing of Lilly & Company.

Understanding the issues reviewed by the U.S. Food & Drug Administration (FDA) "contrary to SEC rules" a company's stock can be downgraded to junk statues. Considering this rating is a value that may be worth millions or billions of dollars especially when the FDA approves an internal medicine or other good, or bad activity concerns that can be recognized as subjective harm, adjustments must be considered by the company. This becomes conditionally relevant to thousands of small investors which includes the employees of the publicly traded company.

A financial definition of "Junk Bond" is a corporate bond with a speculative credit rating of BB or lower by Standard & Poor's and Moody's rating systems. These are junk bonds issued by companies without long term track records of sales and earnings, or by those with questionable credit strength. Since junk bonds are more volatile and pay higher yields than "investment grade" bonds (c/o stocks), many people trading them are part of as risk-oriented investors. This is usually a process of research to specialize in trading these investment items as securities for their high quality, and greenmail cash effect. Institutions of finance with "fiduciary" responsibilities are not supposed to by junk bonds due to these risk factors. Therefore the FDA, the U.S. Department of Agriculture, and others even with certain Securities & Exchange Commission issues can cause good, and conditionally bad repercussions within the logical or lawful activity of a company's stocks, bonds, and their vital business activity.

Coming out of the 1930s America observed the concern that various businesses could not be trusted or were overly trusted until certain laws were established. This was a matter upon which more so consisted of how the banks, and investment banks would affect the industrial base of businesses as well. After the establishment of the U.S. Securities and Exchange Commission following the Great Depression various U.S. Defense contractors such as U.S. Steel Corporation (USS), Zenith Corporation, General Electric Corp (GE), and Motorola Inc. were businesses seeking new technology, and advancements. This consisted of research, product development, and economics that the United States government considered important to investors, and the American general public.

Contrary to government contracts, various labor unions in America were becoming a movement for better wages, safety concerns, and benefits like workman's compensation due to injuries, and sometimes death on the job. Within funding corporate mergers on some occasions the workman's compensation argument was just as fierce with some relief in 1970. Starting throughout the 1970s these labor conditions became vital issues of "law and industry" that had to be addressed for safety, and economic concerns. Then also in 1970 workman's compensation was established as federal law with the Williams-Striger "Occupational Safety and Health Act" (OSHA) that created workplace safety regulation. Later in a separate industry concern the Mine Safety and Health Administration Act (MSHA) detailed out regulation for certain occupations like coal mining which became a demanding commodity for industries such as energy, and steel manufacturing throughout America. Therefore observing some of these companies effected by coal mining accidents occasionally they changed corporate business hands of ownership with conditional mergers, and buyouts as well.

Observing the vast amount of coal mining companies that have been part of a buyout or merger transition is slightly tremendous with delicate, and some aggressive debates, and or arguments. Most large energy oriented public utility, and steel companies such as U.S. Steel Corporation, and LTV Steel Corporation have shared part ownership in various coal mining, and production businesses.

Today during 2011 Massey Energy, and International Coal Group are two of the largest coal production businesses in America. These companies are somewhat idol or secluded with vital responsibilities to the fact that when tensions flare up after certain coal mining accidents the business including liability of all operating procedures, and conditions occasionally becomes debatable. These are active coal mining values with MSHA concerns which are important issues to the disciplines of the coal mining industry, and workplace safety concerns throughout America. Therefore this commodity has importance that preserves the life line of most energy values in most all parts of America, but with conditional awareness.

Considering various large and small items that most United States Defense contractors have provided, as procurements, there is a logical concept of inflation, and even deflation, upon which these businesses had to seek logical "economic and legal balance" from. To establish a profit with a logical balance sheet of bookkeeping this also increased the value of some businesses, and corporations. This consisted of the diversified prices within sales of products, and services to the American system of local, state, and more so the federal government with the U.S. Constitution and people in mind. These concerns are vital and applicable to banking, and investment banking business products, and more so services which has been a strong part of the economic determination of business liquidity growth in various businesses. Concerning issues about a vast amount of businesses with labor, and management expenses most good business leaders with discipline started to take closer notice at inflation, and certain banking conflicts. These issues of conflict became very serious during the recession of 2000. This was the process of moving into an economic, and social recovery with new laws that most of these businesses or corporations followed as important details.

All of these corporate businesses, and their employees depended on banking, and some even more so investment banking. This includes some mergers or buyouts that are similar to corporations with the entire banking industry depending on government loans, bonds, policy values, and regulation. Considering this the rules had to be appropriately understood, and applied. Also these businesses where becoming a supervised level of control by the Glass Steagall Act, and the U.S. expanding disciplines of the Federal Reserve Bank system. These economic issues become important to restrain the level of economic, and more so banking values during the 1920s period of deflation. Therefore if offering people a job (c/o 1929-30) was a conflicting issue, certainly buying an additional business you would think had to be a server conflict as well. Actually the number of buyout/merger transactions which have expanded business properly with help from government, and the American people occasionally became more progressive.

An interesting and critical resource of corporate mergers and buyouts in America from the 1950s up to 2011 has been with various highly secured corporations manufacturing defense, aerospace, and or consumer products. These corporations such as General Electric Corporation, Lockheed Martin Inc, Northrop Corporation (c/o Northrop Grumman Corp), and the Raytheon Corporation are businesses that on occasions buy other businesses or merge with different product divisions they find useful. General Electric Corporation has been fairly astute in their buying and sale agreements of corporate businesses, and certain product divisions within the tenure's of Jack Welch, and presently Jeffery Immelt. This format of business transactions has made General Electric Corporations a more productive conglomerate which consisted of a certain amount of high and low managing employees keeping this diversified business logical.

Under the tenure of Jack Welch whom retired from GE Corp in 2001 his objective to buy, and sale businesses and corporate divisions was a tremendous task that people like Jeffery Immelt followed, and this somewhat became one of the GE ways of expansion. This has included GE Corp. buying RCA (c/o NBC), upon which the NBC television network (c/o 1986), then partnering with MSNBC & Microsoft became a competitive, and productive venture. Other transactions included the purchase of a struggling Montgomery Ward's Corp as a GE Capital subsidiary, and the Instrumentarium dental products from the UK buyout which is

1 of many GE Healthcare purchases. From there it seems GE has manufactured, and sold State-of-the-Art radiology equipment from these transactions. Other buyouts consisted of the likes of Dillard's Department stores credit unit also being bought by General Electric. Also GE Water Technologies buyout of Zenon Environmental Systems for $758 million dollars with various others to the tune of 6 acquisitions in 2004, 1 acquisition in 2005, 3 acquisitions in 2006, and 4 acquisitions in 2007 before the most recent U.S. financial crisis.

A vast amount of General Electric merger/buyout activity became logical business concerns occasionally managed by GE Capital. This factor included a format of other subsidiaries, and business divisions within the structure of the General Electric Corporation. Then at the General Electric Corp they also sold assets such as a computer division to Honeywell (c/o 1970) which was a spin-off of Genigraphics Corporation. During the following years GE Aerospace Division was sold to Martin Marietta (c/o becoming Lockheed Martin), which then they folded on Montgomery Ward's, and sold GE Advanced Materials to Apollo Management for $3.8 billion dollars. General Electric Corp during 2011 completed the sale of NBC Universal with Comcast Corp becoming the shareholders with a majority ownership, upon which General Electric Corp still owned a 48% stake of the joint venture. Also these business transactions of expanding business (c/o even GE Jet Engines or Light Bulbs & Lighting Systems) is how they put additional value into their corporation like parts of a puzzle. Therefore this even occasionally became the concept of their (GE) set up of manufacturing products in certain other foreign countries.

Raytheon Corporation, Northrop Grumman Corporation, General Dynamics Corp., the "BF" Goodrich Corporation, and Lockheed Martin Corporation are also considered astute within a format of strong American corporations. These valued corporate businesses have merger, buyout, and business disciplines that appropriate progressive economic transitions to the American economy. Upon most good, and bad disciplines, or opinions these are corporations that operate worldwide, and therefore on occasions they

businesses which has been one of the more severe issues of intent to be slightly on the side of greed similar to an investment bank, and not logical corporate business.

The format of these business issues with problems throughout the American societies economy, workforce, and the resources of other businesses has caused severe setbacks that will take vital time to correct. This applies to when corporations such as Enron dictated various smaller more productive businesses similar to Portland General Electric which is a public utility company in the state of Oregon. Some Portland GE employees watched their company pension accounts go from over $100,000.00 to less than $5,000.00 or worse in value. This took Enron 5 years to severely harm the economic stability within what took these Portland GE employees over 20 years to establish. These transactions that provided hopeful concerns of a good outline to the American economy were regulated by the Securities and Exchange Commission which were slightly late to correct the problems caused by Enron. Therefore the Enron conflict left this public utility company in the hands of a destructive corporate business process of businesspeople, and then by law Portland GE had to be restructured.

After the future of the Enron Corporation was discovered to be disastrous the potential business liquidity, and equity they had acquired within other businesses where forced into serious economic, and financial conflict. These newly founded problems consisted of the original, and newly added employees within banking institutions to be hit hard along with Citigroup Incorporated that had to restructure from Enron, and other severe American issues. Now Citigroup is suffering with economic problems that are almost as bad as Bank of America whom today during 2011 is at the possible point of being removed from the New York Stock Exchange. Therefore this conditional fact means that these banks (c/o other businesses) would operate as a private company or be bought out with a stronger concept of liquidity. Upon this problem becoming worse (c/o Bank of America) this would eliminate their stock shares being trading on one of the major stock exchanges; if they survive in business overall.

The Enron Corporation was started by the merger of Houston Natural Gas Co, and InterNorth Gas Company of Omaha which included their 37,000 miles of gas pipeline. Kenneth Lay the founder of Enron Corporation was a former executive of the Houston Natural Gas Company, but after 26 years his establishment of Enron could not maintain without various activities of fraud. This was a problem to the employees, and various worldwide business issues when they tried to expand as most productive, and lawful businesses and corporations do. Therefore this became a considerable factor of why their losses came to over $70 billion dollars. This occurred at Enron during their factual dispute of bankruptcy after 2001, and with some corporate activity and certain buyouts causing conflicts to the U.S. financial system being out of control.

During the same time apart from Enron, the WorldCom Corporation had seen a few good, bad, or what was considered interesting days with various mergers. The WorldCom Corporation after 20 years of business then failed with them losing $180 billion dollars evaporating into nothing. WorldCom bought out half a dozen communication companies upon which then they were established as IDB WorldCom. Then they established a $37 billion dollar merger with MCI making them MCI WorldCom. Following this two years later in 1999 WorldCom and Sprint Corporation put together a merger valued at $115 billion dollars which was disapproved by United States and European regulators as non-workable, and or illegal. Taking this type of corporate merger under consideration this was an anti-trust law concern with businesses making financial agreements to become the largest or controlling business in certain industry concerns.

After what seems, and existed to be an insecure and out of control merger, and buyout collaboration of issues and equity by the WorldCom Corporation, they ended up laying off 6,000 workers in 2001. Then 17,000 lay-offs followed in 2002 with the resignation of its founder, and CEO Bernard Ebbers. Bernard Ebbers was summoned to testify to the U.S. Congress, and he took the fifth amendment action of not disclosing his business involvement. Therefore these matters were taken under negative consideration, by various members of Congress, and then thru the federal courts proceedings of filing on the matter Bernard Ebbers was prosecuted, and sentenced to 25 years in federal prison. It's important to remember that WorldCom was not a brokerage firm, but theoretically they were a :"Communications Company" and therefore they should have kept their work discipline in that business sector capacity without crossing the line of anti-trust law concerns.

Considering these corporate merger and buyout issues with good, bad, and occasionally destructive values within business transactions, the American society still has private companies, and professional offices that are productively important. A certain amount of these professional businesses are large engineering, architecture, and accounting firms including hospitals that usually have helpful disciplines to the American society. As this applies to various financial brokerage firms a vast amount of them are going public to sale their stocks on the trading floors of various financial market exchanges. Understanding this, more businesses are seeking financial investments from the diversified investors of America. Contrary to this trillions of investment dollars have been loss to fraudulent business. Also these companies that are occasionally publicly offered on various stock exchanges has become a process for banks, and brokerage firms to target corporate greed concerns, and act as corporate raiders. This level of business is factual within their own interest and ambition to control various businesses. Therefore this was a severe, and long-term factual problem upon how any corrections would restructure the American society of business with an economic equation for the people.

Some of these businesses contrary to corporate raiders have opportunities of maybe receiving an attractive liquidation offer similar to the one Bear Stearns provided. This was the tremendous logic of the Bear Stearns investment company being bought out by J.P. Morgan Chase in March of 2008. The Bear Stearns Co. Inc. had suffered tuff times during 2007, and 2008 upon which their 52 week stock price high was $133.20 a share before the crisis hit, and the J.P. Morgan Co. bought-out the 85 year old company for $2.00 dollars a share. This is one of the sad issues within what happens to various companies that fail, and this considerably looks like a predator, or a savor has come to pick up the inexpensive peace's that remained to understand any possible future value.

As various brokerage firms buy low, and sale high it seems that they have put their own profession in the same category. Observing Bear Stearns, Enron, WorldCom, hundreds of banks, and others whose assets were left seized by the FBI, and or were auctioned off these assets were part of the victim's, and plaintiffs compensation. These issues that lingered where to be purchased by people, and more so companies that could afford them. Other than the Bear Stearns issue, Lehman Brothers suffered tremendous problems during the same time frame throughout the 2008 financial market turmoil within an overall economic, and financial crisis. The concept of Lehman Brothers, and the U.S. economic crisis which consisted of hundreds of banks, and their association with mortgage backed securities became a foreclosed property crisis in America.

The problem within the U.S. economy failing to the extent of people's homes, and business properties being threatened by foreclosure was a vital conflict. Both Bear Stearns, and more so Lehman Brothers including their 1984 merger activity with American Express, numerous corporate mergers, initial public offerings, and other stable brokerage activity was part of their business process that was overcome by losses. These were the tremendous losses in the mortgage banking industry. Also the September 11, 2001 terror attacks was also a tremendous conflict to their business though the mortgage lenders did not lose as many people fatally. These are rational issues within the American society that instigate, manipulate, or perpetuate conflicts within business values that affect the people, and economic progress. Although various things happen in America and from the observation of its system of government, we do seek opportunities to improve their social values to help future years of hopeful progress, and economic stability.

CHAPTER TWO
THE AMERICAN ECONOMY WITH GOOD AND BAD MERGERS

Throughout the American society of public, and private businesses including corporations on most relevant occasions, various business matters consist of corporate mergers which can be valuable if they are pursued properly with productive resources. This also consist of relevant concerns within observation from the Securities and Exchange Commission, certain Attorney Generals, and other regulators such as the Anti-Trust division of the United States Department of Justice. Then the American system of government, and the people can adjust to the issue of what may be considered a good, or bad merger with agreements. This from time to time outlines the diversified effects over time that applies a money circulation, and adjustments to the Gross Domestic Product (GDP) as it applies to the U.S. economy. Also this becomes an issue recognized more so by individual states with regional economic concerns throughout the United States, and therefore long term commitments become valuable.

Understanding businesses that establish corporate mergers this becomes a process that the businesspeople involved must be responsible for within terms of a commitment. In addition this may include or consist of hard work, and their discipline of leveraging to combine production of various business products, and managed assets with other concerns in a workable business capacity. Usually the merger is a consolidation of business sectored interest, and asset management control as it applies to the majority stake holders within equity. Considering this, the larger the corporation or firm is with subsidiary businesses, products, and service divisions, this has and can provide a logical, and lawful format to support a structure of discipline for progress within a business.

Observing the term's corporate merger, and corporate buyout there are similarities, and issues that come under the rules of the stake holder, and or the majority stock holder which is part of the management's decision of consolidation. This can, and dose become the parent company that consist of one or more subsidiary businesses with an equation of what is observed or considered as an industry leader, or a strong productive corporate or business value of discipline. General Electric Corporation (GE) has spent the last 25 years (c/o 1986 to 2011) as the parent company of National Broadcasting Company (NBC) as an important subsidiary. Contrary to GE Corp, NBC also is an industry leader in television programming. NBC is also partly owned by "RCA" Corp (the Radio Corporation of America) that has been around for decades, and upon which they were somewhat established slightly before television. Therefore this industry with various businesses has changed with advancements.

General Electric Corporation did expand in the business merger/buyout of RCA and their intentional target of NBC with the arbitration of cable television broadcasting. Jack Welch the CEO of General Electric Corp lead this buyout and merger agreement with NBC, and Microsoft as an expanded resource of cable television. This then lead 3 businesses to establish a network which became a productive issue of expansion of "TV and the Internet" as MSNBC. Considering these merger, and business matters certain subjects where becoming market issues of value in America, and around the world. Some of these business resources go back 100 years between General Electric Corp, Westinghouse Electric Corp, and the American Telephone & Telegraph Corp as it applies to certain businesses. These were conditionally established as business agreements with RCA

Corporation (c/o NBC), and even the United States Department of Defense. This even includes issues from the Anti-Trust division of the U.S. Department of Justice, and the Communication Act of 1934 establishing the Federal Communication Commission.

Understanding some complexity of industry specialist or leaders in most corporate business concerns, these diversified mergers were becoming vitally important to observe. This is the logic to know the various values of a defined merger; which is a combination of two or more companies, either through "pooling of interest sectors" or where accounts are combined. Another factor is a purchase, where the amount paid over and above the acquired company's book value (with real or possible debt) is carried on the books of the purchaser as goodwill. In the same equation a consolidation can exist where a new company is formed to acquire the net assets of the combining companies. With distinction, and strictly speaking only a combination in which one of the companies survive as a legal entity are called mergers or, more formerly, statutory mergers; thus consolidations, or statutory consolidations. On occasions these are technically not mergers, though the term merger is commonly applied to them.

Mergers meeting the legal criteria for pooling of interest and business sectors, where common stock is exchanged for common stock, are nontaxable and are called tax-free mergers. Where an acquisition takes place by the purchase of assets or stock using cash or a debt instrument for payment, the merger is a taxable capital gain to the selling company or its stockholders. There is a potential benefit to such taxable purchase acquisitions, however, in that the acquiring company can write up the acquired company's assets by the amount by which the market value exceeds the book value; that difference can then be charged off to depreciation with a resultant tax saving.

The business or corporate merger process can be classified in at least five terms appropriated to their economic function. The first is a "horizontal merger" which is one combining direct competitors in the same product lines and markets. Second is a "vertical merger" which combines customers and companies or suppliers and the company.

Third is a market extension merger which combines companies selling the same product in different markets. Forth is a "product extension merger" that combines companies selling different but related products in the same market. Fifth is a conglomerate merger which combines companies with none of these other common or above stated business relationships or similarities. These business or corporate merger issues including statutory issues of legislature, and law also apply to the term acquisition. Understanding the format of a corporate acquisition is relevant to one company taking over the controlling interest in another company. Investors are always looking out for companies that are likely to be acquired, because those who want to acquire such companies are often willing to pay more than the (SEC regulated) market price for the outstanding or controlling shares, that the purchasing company needs to complete the acquisition.

An American merger between the Goodrich Corporation and Uniroyal Inc. (formerly the United States Rubber Company est. 1882) consisted of American factory workers, and the changing times in America's cycle of manufacturing, and economic disciplines with conflicts. Considering this combined merger within Uniroyal and Goodrich during 1986 this was an acquisition of hopeful expansion with Goodrich Corporation as the controlling company. The Goodrich Corporation (c/o formerly BF Goodrich) had a productive business providing the sales of high performance tires, and rubber fabrication products. Considering Goodrich Corp. with the good, and bad of the American economy, some of their "aircraft tire and brake system" business was economically sound (c/o certain aerospace & defense contracts) until they observed a change within their competitor of Uniroyal (Inc.) that went private during 1986.

Taking concern of this observation both Uniroyal and Goodrich made a consolidated effort to become the Uniroyal Goodrich Tire Company in a merger agreement. Upon various values both of these corporations consisted of a merger with consolidated equality to advance American tire products with additional earnings, equity, and liquidity that could expand business productions between the two as one business. Contrary to this hopeful ambition the merger was considered too complex, and in 1988 Goodrich Co. sold its 50% stake in the Uniroyal Co to Clayton & Dubilier of New York, and then soon after Uniroyal was sold to Michelin a "French Company". This is part of America's bout with global business which all evaluated citizens, and executives must be competitive with logical values.

After the sale of Uniroyal Inc. the BF Goodrich "Company" had established its self out of the tire business. Then from there they pursued various acquisition's to help expand their chemicals, and aerospace business. They then bought Rohr Inc. that manufactures aerospace jet engine casings which expanded them into the aircraft components industry. During the year 1999 BF Goodrich acquired Coltec Industries for $2.2 billion dollars in stock, and assumed debt. This expanded their business to become the No. 1 supplier of aircraft landing gear, and other aircraft manufactured parts. Today with their CEO Marshall Larsen of the Goodrich Corporation they are expanding worldwide with a new plant in Poland, although their headquarters is in Charlotte, North Carolina apart from the founding establishment in Akron, Ohio. This transition is where America on occasions has changed with the times, and has recognized various industry concerns throughout a vast amount of corporations. These are the decisions that the best resource of conditions within management will be evaluated by, and with understanding about most up to date business concerns including government with various tax issues, and other societal values.

Good corporate management becomes just as vital as the entry level of employees, or labor union members who learn, and become productive in various small, or large businesses or corporations. The business resource of the Goodyear Corporation, and BF Goodrich Corporation whom had sold tires to airline transportation companies, and automobile companies has concerns that affected the U.S. market of airline companies. This becomes the issue were inflation such as within the oil industry has a similar effect from tire manufactures if they can control, and maintain their quarterly and annual earnings.

During April of 2001 American Airlines Incorporated agreed to a merger with Trans World Airlines (TWA) which consolidated their large combination of corporate assets, and businesses. TWA and its holding company Trans World Airline Corporation were struggling in its own part of 3 bankruptcy filings in ten years due to conflicts with the Chairman Charles Tillinghast Jr., and his effort to give in to lower earnings. This became drastic upon which the company had observed these bankruptcy concerns as vital factors of importance. Other issues in TWA conflicts consisted of a strong interest of majority ownership from two corporate raiders. Those corporate raiders where Frank Lorenzo, and then the more aggressive bidder, and corporate raider Carl Icahn.

Observing the board of directors at TWA Carl Ichan was their choice, "but soon after", his conflicting work was becoming a downfall for the TWA business operation, and most future concerns. These decisions from Carl Icahn in 1985 whom bought into TWA during a time of crisis was evident to how far you can trust some corporate raiders, their decisions, and even the lawful extent of their money invested. The corporate raider activity of Carl Icahn did not seem to help the company restructure, but more so made decisions that consisted of negative, and conflicting transactions. During Carl Icahn's activity at TWA he sold off most of its valuable assets which drove TWA into deeper debt, and then bankruptcy in 1992 upon which in 1993 TWA's board members eliminated Carl Icahn's involvement. Sense the 1970s this has been a problem to various airline companies in these sectored business markets of America that have suffered tremendously. Besides auto, tire, and even airline companies that consist of large ticket items these business concerns have suffered with additional high cost issues of conflict. Therefore bankruptcy is an indicated reliable factor within junk bond business values of consideration.

During the 1970s and 1980s more and more airline businesses were troubled by fuel cost, conflicting management, labor issues, and Middle East terrorist providing threats, and active conflicts. On occasions one airline company may have suffered worse than others from various complex issues, but the industry had vital reason to be on logical alert concerning "the aircraft hi-jacking" years before. TWA was a business that suffered from a variation of issues before

American Airlines Corporation upon which whom observed this "junk bond" valued company as an opportunity of advancement. This became their chance to expand their present business progress that started between 1925 and 1930 lasting until 1992. After 1992 the saddest of their days occurred in 1995 thru 2001. These days consisted of conflicts with Charles Tillinghast Jr. the Chairman of TWA (c/o Trans World Airlines Corp) for the duration of those years which excepting, and managing an additional bankruptcy filing was one of their merger agreements with American Airline Corporation.

What made the TWA, and American Airlines Corp a merger of consolidated discipline is the fact that TWA had become established as a business of responsible liquidity within their activity as an airline transportation company for decades. The Chairman and CEO of American Airlines Inc. was Donald Carty whom is the person who helped structure the business merger transaction with Trans World Airlines Corp for the controlling stake, and buyout in TWA. Considering their established level of equity American Airlines Inc. spent $500 million dollars to purchase TWA, and assumed $2 billion dollars in liabilities which was responsive to the American society of consumers, business, and the government. The loss of TWA flight 800 during 1996 with the death of 230 passengers was another sad issue, and this caused a setback for this company. Considering these factors the company, TWA had tremendous conflicts of survival or possible restructuring that did not work, but American Airlines Inc. found useful assets in TWA until American Airlines had a slight restructuring from their losses on September 11, 2001.

As America observed business progress during the 1990s, certain conflicts including government failures has taken a vast amount of American businesses backwards from prosperous growth. TWA was only one of a variety of businesses that loss ground in the format of expansion, and business survival throughout America. American Airlines Inc. suffered severely from the September 11, 2001 terrorist attacks with additional threats, and this included the U.S. Department of Homeland Security (c/o TSA with the FAA), working to appropriate certain levels of safety after these destructive terrorist attacks. Contrary to this logic within the George Bush, and Bill Clinton presidential administration's the fact of international investments with international terror had again become a vital concern. Middle East conflicts during the early 1990s had critical U.S. National Security concerns. The Airline industry, and the Oil industry in America are most times worldwide businesses, but the oil industry seems to be the least effected along with companies like Microsoft Corp or Goldman Sachs Group Inc.

Contrary to the losses at the New York World Trade Center's observing the 9-11 terrorist attacks a vast amount of American corporations have seem to be considered for various merger transactions to survive in business or control certain markets. Considering a certain amount of business mergers that were not part of the September 11, 2001 crisis, other business mergers where pursued by people from, and committed to making the best ally decisions possible from other countries. Rupert Murdoch, and Lakshmi Mittal are two businesspeople whom acquired American corporate assets which had been around for at least a century. The observation of Rupert Murdoch the Chairman and CEO of News Corporation who was born into the newspaper business in Australia has established control of a small fraction of news media market businesses in America. Understanding this evaluation of these two individuals, and maybe a few others this consisted of how the U.S. government will except or discipline their newly corporate owned, and operated (c/o Satellite, News, and other) technology business matters.

During 2005 Rupert Murdoch acquired his third newspaper from a corporate business buyout which was the Dow Jones & Company acquisition upon whom publishes the Wall Street Journal, and Barron's financial newspaper apart from his corporate ownership of other businesses. This buyout cost him in the range of $5 billion dollars. Also this purchase brought him to own at least three American newspapers which he began buying in 1973, contrary to some media businesses he started, or those he owns that exist in other countries. Additional acquisitions he pursued consisted of the San Antonio Express-News (1973), and the New York Post (1976) being his larger part, and pursuit of merger activity to expand his News Corp business, and how this increased a level of his wealth. Rupert Murdoch, and his merger activities as a billionaire has existed with various rulings by the Federal Communication Commission (FCC) considering that he also bought the "Fox Television and News Network", including other satellite and communication business holdings.

Lakshmi Mittal whom was born in India has acquired a controlling amount of steel manufactures in America, and a few other countries. Observing the ArcelorMittal business concerns during the first decade of 2002 they have gained control of business in the U.S., and International steel industry which was from a combination of buyout/merger issues within certain former steel companies throughout America, and then Europe. Those companies under his merger/buyout control are (c/o International Steel Group) Inland Steel Corporation, LTV Steel Corporation, and Bethlehem Steel Corporation. Bethlehem Steel Corporation was one of the last newly built steel factories observing the 1950s, 60s, and 70s.

During most American wars these steel companies were considered as important U.S. Defense contractors. As Lakshmi Mittal has pursued merger/buyout issues in other countries leveraging 10s of billions of dollars to invest in other steel mill operations, the Midwest of the United States have loss, or reorganized a vast amount of U.S. Defense contractors. These ArcelorMittal acquisition's started as Ispat International whom bought out Inland Steel Company in 1998. Also this process then included Bethlehem Steel Corporation whom conditionally filed for bankruptcy in 2001. Then International Steel Group (ISG) with Wilber Ross acquired the Bethlehem Steel Corporation with its conflicting losses. Following these transactions in time ISG agreed to a merger with Mittal Steel before they spent in access of an estimated $40 billion dollars on Arcelor of Europe to become ArcelorMittal Steel whom somewhat operates worldwide.

Throughout other parts of the United States these issues of corporate mergers, and buyouts are recognized by the U.S. government for a variation of national security concerns. One of the most complex arguments was pursued by William Donaldson whom offered conflicts against a somewhat hidden or conflicting business called Quest Communications Corporation. Also within additional arguments the U.S. Senator from North Dakota; Byron Dorgan also provided harsh criticism to the CEO of this *Quest Corp for not being astute about his corporate business, and the federal laws. Observing a variation of U.S. National Security concerns this issue with other conditions had been held a bit low on the U.S. National Defense agenda, but any communications company that operates in the U.S. must reserve the Constitutional rights of law binding citizens, and their activities of productive business including social concerns. Considering this, the priority list of National Security issues during the late 1990s, and the activity of the U.S. federal government did not make the best decisions on proper reviews about various international executives with "Defense" contract work. Due to these supporting conflicts that may have more interest in Mexico, and the Middle East then the United States job opportunities and national security became vital concerns.

The issues of good and bad foreign relations in America was considered with caution to apply additional security upon which also American National Security after 2001 was adjusted with aggressive values of importance. These concerns for American values included some regional citizens, and or employees who observed various issues within the loss of American business owners. Another effect was the slowdown of various other American citizens as businesspeople to expand their existing business or create good productive issues as a new startup business. These were issues, and concerns that where sometimes not taken serious by the state or federal government when American people applied these issues as vital complaints.

The U.S. Attorney General's within Janet Reno, John Ascroft, and then Alberto Gonzales with their U.S. Anti-Trust divisions, and investigators lacked lawful conditional duties as it applies to certain U.S. Securities and Exchange Commission concerns. This was even more so critical during the Bill Clinton administration which the Attorney Generals were part of a group of people that became insecure for the prosperous values of certain small businesses, and investors trying to expand. The American U.S. Constitutional values of prosperity and domestic tranquility where crumbling for a small length of time. This was the concern that they will occasionally help improve investment opportunities, and prosecute diversified people of wealth whom don't have good intensions to be lawful proprietors in various markets. Contrary to this delay of discipline, others within their business or government concerns of being ambitious people as lawful American potential business owners were subjected to severe losses. Between the leadership of Harvey Pitt, and Arthur Levitt they seem to lack responsible enforcement of vital U.S. Constitutional values which apply to the laws of the Securities and Exchange Commission. Therefore their staff had seem to be misguided on valuable SEC complaints which sometimes became severely diversified after financial losses were severe.

Within the U.S. Attorney General's office (c/o the 1990s thru 2000s), and the Anti-Trust division of the U.S. Department of Justice, certain parts of a bad market within resources has become slightly complacent to the American economy. An enormous amount of banking institutions found themselves with lending conflicts that in hardly no way would work long-term in the American society. Just as banking institutions found, and created mortgage investments with very little value, bad Mortgage Backed Securities affected a large percentage of the banking industry, and small investors. The banking industry throughout the United States from 2009 up thru 2011 has suffered tremendous bank failure issues with only a few being bought out by other banks. The numbers are severe with the Federal Deposit Insurance Corporation (FDIC) observing depository control within the failure of 25 banks in 2008, 140 banks in 2009, 157 banks in 2010, and more than 38 banks in 2011. Observing this the banking industry from 2007 thru 2010 have been the timing factor for the highest level of risk within any business or a bank to buy or merge with another bank. In general, a certain value of economic logic has occurred with these bank businesses which have accumulated a "Junk Bond" level rating value whether stocks or bonds are offered, or not.

The logic and problem with mortgages and even sub-prime mortgages with their association applied to mortgage backed securities that have failed in most all 50 states during the 1st decade of 2000, have conditionally become a tremendous economic issue, and social problem. The magnitude of this problem consisted of a complex real estate market struggling to achieve economic, and financial values of business liquidity. This format of these issues have been a newly reconsolidated investment level of products offered by investment banks which have ventured into the business process of small local real estate business investors. These small and occasionally large business investors usually have a way of carefully making a property buy or sale agreement which is transitioned into a banking and consumer issue of value. Then investors and some small businesses seeking liquidity throughout local community markets of commercial, and residential real estate property with investments may include issues of renovation, property taxes, and ownership increased values. Therefore within local business people with citizen responsibilities competing against large banks that failed everybody suffered a loss. Then we understand that some rental property disciplines should not have been disturbed in a destructive legal, and or financial capacity.

As mortgage or business lending investments applies to investment banks, Bear Stearns (founded in 1923) upon approaching 2008 had a 52 week valued high of $133.20 per share, and before that the stock price had once exceeded $160.00 a share in 2007. After their failure on march 2, 2008 the investment bank Bear Stearns signed an agreement to merge, and be bought out by J.P. Morgan Chase for $10.00 a share, apart from its market value price of $2.00 a share. Observing the Bear Stearns failure, this became the resource of having a merger value of about $1.2 billion dollars in the complete transaction, upon which other brokerage firms hold properties with good and bad investment issues of concern. This was clearly one vital issue of how mortgage backed securities throughout America affected most small, and large business owners, investors, and citizens.

Lehman Brothers was another investment banking business that suffered tremendous economic problems in 2008. During the month of September 2008 the company Lehman Brothers holding Inc.

filed for chapter 11 bankruptcy protection. This was an investment brokerage company that was established in 1850 by the family of brothers; Henry, Emanuel, and Mayer Lehman over a vast amount of decades. They at one time where the 4th largest investment bank in the United States behind Goldman Sachs, Morgan Stanley, and Merrill Lynch. The Lehman Brothers Holding Incorporated format of business has also been involved in a merger in the American Express Company. This merger created Shearson Lehman/American Express which in 1988 became Shearson Lehman Hutton Inc. that was part of E.F. Hutton & Company becoming involved in this vertical merger. A year later in 1989 they supported F. Ross Johnson's management team in a competitive bidding buyout for RJR Nabisco. They were outbid by Kohlberg Kravis Roberts & Company whom had supportive backing by Drexel Burnham Lambert. Therefore the process they knew very well became part of their concept of failing within the observation of a supportive rescue from J.P. Morgan Chase, whom has been involved in various mergers themselves.

These became the times when investment banks where recognized with troubling hard times, and some computer product corporations with innovative levels of diversification. This valued concern was seen with tremendous prosperity from selling their products, and with companies going thru various changes. Considering the American system of investment bank corporate underwriting of stock offering for a company, in the 1950s Lehman Brothers Inc. managed an initial public offering (IPO) of Digital Equipment Corp. This IPO which consisted of an underwritten value for Digital Equipment Corp to raise investment dollars established this company financially, and professionally. This made them a prime U.S. computer industry leader upon which then they were able to expand in the newly established markets for computer networking programs. Their computer product development values consisted of various computer systems, software, and peripherals which was helpful to telephone modems, and networking computer systems. Some of these products were room sized computer (input-output) server systems. Their minicomputers where considered astute for scientific, and engineering subject activities during the 1970s, and 1980s. In June of 1998 Digital Equipment Corporation was purchased by Compaq Computer Corporation, and their Hudson, Massachusetts (Digital Eq.) compiler manufacturing facility was sold to the Intel Corporation.

Compaq Computer Corporation was started from 3 upper level managers formerly of Texas Instruments investing $1,000.00 each. These founders of Compaq Computer Corporation were Rod Canion, Jim Harris, and Bill Murto whom involved themselves with people from other computer hardware manufactures between IBM Corporation, and Intel Corporation. These conditional resources established appropriate success between what was Digital Equipment Corporation, and Compaq Computer Corporation being sold to Hewlett-Packard Company for $25 billion dollars. This transaction was argued as unfavorable by a few people with disagreeable concerns. Then upon this fact it also consisted of a severe public proxy battle by shareholders, and Walter Hewlett. Upon all the good, and occasional bad the Hewlett Packard Company has expanded its computer base with fairly good sales which increased their liquidity holdings as a company. This level of expansion has given them potential to be a lead competitor against companies such as Dell Computer Corporation, and even Apple Computer Incorporate.

CHAPTER THREE
HOSTILE TAKEOVERS AND CORPORATE RAIDERS

||||||||||||||||||||||||||||||||||||||||||||||||||||||||||||||||||||

Throughout America the issue of corporate hostile takeover concerns of a corporation, and or the business capacity of investors, and people with ownership values have provided opinions that are vitally important to understand, and evaluate. This has become a business transaction process that sense the 1980s, and 1990s government has created various legislature to control what is similar to anti-trust law conflicts. As corporate raiders are involved, the attempt to take-over a corporation with a person or corporation having more or less money, and or leveraging power then the target companies invested interest, this usually exist with likes, or dislikes.

Importantly the public information of a corporation occasionally is most times outlined in various proxy statement reports. Understanding that "the Proxy Statement" is required by U.S. federal law, certain conditions must be considered, and outlined as corporate business procedures. With these legal disciplines the U.S. government concerning the issues of the company, and the board of directors are lawfully disclosed. Therefore various activities by the publicly held corporation are provided to the shareholders to have a lawful understanding of most all logical public business matters.

Various hostile takeover opinions also exist within the concern that a corporate raider can "help" or take away the most valued levels of sacrifices of business expansion. Also in some concern American born corporate raiders are 90% more valuable than foreign business people buying American businesses. Contrary to this conflict the businesses that can't agree on a profitable, and or productive direction which includes U.S. and or international business becomes an overall problem. This problem will affect a level of discipline for other people ready to make vital decisions effecting, or supporting the corporation. The General Electric Corporation with Jack Welch, and a few corporations like General Dynamics Corp, AM General Corp, Lockheed Martin, and even "Raytheon Corporation with their present CEO William Swanson" are businesses that have managed this format of a transition properly. T-Boone Pickens, and Carl Icahn have made these decisions with the observation of soliciting American investment shareholders of various corporate business issues. Therefore these business concerns can be found conditionally in new, and or older existing businesses that have at various times consisted of worthwhile productive levels of business progress.

These issues of corporate raider activity by people such as T-Boone Pickens, Carl Icahn, Reginald Lewis, and a few others have consisted of greenmail economic accumulated factors of additional cash liquidity. This is also part of their control of a corporations stock from their investments. It can also be recognized within the formal issues of one corporation seeking control of another corporate conditional business resource. This creates a transition of ownership which sometimes consist of investment banking arbitration, and occasionally individuals that are excepted with the corporation's board of directors. In all productive business values this is part of how a small business becomes a productively expanding corporation.

The concept of arbitration with other investors had become an exceptional level of business activity that Reginald Lewis pursued within his acquisition, and buyout of Beatrice International Foods. Reginald Lewis (c/o TLC) was a scaled back corporate raider (financier) due in part to his profession as a corporate lawyer. He was the first black American to head a U.S. corporation as both the

Chairman & CEO with a majority of stock ownership upon which his company generated over a billion dollars a year. His business ventures of progress started with the McCall Pattern Company. This was a small company that sales home sewing materials, and equipment which he became active in to restructure the company. With leverage buyout assistance from Michael Milken of Drexel Burnham Lambert, Reginald Lewis purchased Beatrice International Foods from the Beatrice Companies for $980 million dollars in 1987.

As Reginald Lewis, and his startup company TLC Beatrice International Holdings Inc had revenue earnings during 1987 of $1.8 billion dollars with additional earning growth in the following years, sadly his health gave out with his untimely death. Reginald Lewis and his work was appreciated by numerous people in various black communities, and with certain other Americans which consisted of good, and bad opinions. Apart from that he did transition various issues into productive business as it applies to what is considered Corporate America. Approaching the 1990s the remaining divisions of Beatrice International Foods Company was acquired by ConAgra Foods Incorporated. ConAgra Foods Inc also pursued leveraged buyouts on various RJR Nabisco brands spending around $400 million dollars. Most of the RJR Nabisco divisions are part of the Kohlberg Kravis Roberts & Company asset spin-off businesses from R.J. Reynolds Tobacco Company which they have controlled sense their buyout in 1988 with argumentative issues of wealth, and product health concerns.

Observing the corporate raider activity of Carl Icahn upon him establishing Icahn & Company which was created as a securities firm observing, and specializing in managing risk arbitrage, and options trading he became active in a vast amount of corporate businesses. This became part of his activity in buying into corporations which on certain occasions has been conditionally aggressive. A vast amount of the corporations that Carl Icahn has purchased consist of a percentage of the stock, and bond holdings in a variation of business/corporate concerns with occasional junk bond ratings. Most times these business/corporate issues are a strong consideration to be restructured within the logic, and format of a corporate merger.

As part of restructuring at Western Union Company, Carl Icahn worked with the President and CEO Robert Amman, and structured a transaction to sale New Valley Corporation to First Financial Management Corporation in a bankruptcy auction for $1.2 billion dollars. A year later in 1995 First Financial Management Corp where Robert Amman became a vice chairman (c/o Icahn as a large bond holder) they then agreed to a $6 billion dollar merger transaction with First Data Corporation whom had the right to spin-off Western Union Company. This spin-off within a logical business procedure was part of making them an independent company to be offered as a publicly traded company.

Business procedures, and transactions such as those at Western Union Co. has put Carl Icahn, and other investors in a position for the lowest purchasing price of stock offered by the restructured Western Union Company. This format of the initial public offering (IPO), and other future business values is how investors make good income from their investments. The Western Union Company improved its business by eliminating telegrams, and offering mostly money gram transfers, which eliminated a bankrupt part it's corporate structure. Distinctively the IPO is almost invariably an opportunity for the existing investors, and even venture capitalist to make big profits considering this is the first time those company stock shares where to be offered in the public investment market. Therefore the company and its investors establish economic growth over a relevant period of time.

Besides the conflicts that Carl Icahn endured at TWA, years later during 2007 Motorola received notice (c/o SEC requirements) that he owns more than 33 million shares of its stock. Also this became factual that he is extremely interested in a seat on Motorola's board as a director. Another Carl Icahn buyout has been observed with Lear Corporation being a target company. The Lear Corporation, and their board of directors had given Icahn approval to by the company for $2.3 billion dollars pending a schedule that was applicable to another possible offer. These are some of the corporate buyouts, and transactions that put Carl Icahn in position for new IPOs in various corporate business conditions that increase an investor, or corporate raiders income, and or earnings of managed liquidity.

Carl Icahn, and T-Boone Pickens had a few things in common such as Phillips Petroleum Company, and a few other companies upon which they held ownership of large amounts of stock. This also includes issues observing that they are two American corporate raiders that have worked to support other Corporate American shareholders within evaluating proxy statement reports that apply to the decisions of various corporate board of directors. These corporate transitional issues are important to observe with future decisions about certain companies on various matters such as stock values, and the future value of business. This also includes the business earning subjects to keep or spin-off various corporate product divisions. Usually both T-Boone Pickens, and Carl Icahn have separate agendas with a strong opinion about various corporate values, and issues, but they both had holdings in Phillips Petroleum. Observing these concerns the oil industry is more of T-Boone Pickens professional discipline as a geologist, and business owner, therefore he became a force with other American shareholders. Therefore this appropriated T-Boone Pickens and other corporate investors and raiders to work towards a buyout of Phillips Petroleum, similar to Carl Icahn with TWA.

Considering T-Boone Pickens was a former Phillips Petroleum employee, years later after him establishing Mesa Petroleum as a productive oil company his new objective was expansion. From there he outlined his concerns with investments to gain control, liquidity, and certain resources to manage the use of existing companies to expand by way of hostile corporate takeovers. In 1981 he completed a buyout of Hougoton Productions Company which was 3 times the size of his Mesa Petroleum business operation. These are values that have guided some of his hostile takeover attempts of Cities Service (Citgo Corp) Gulf Oil, Phillips Petroleum, and Unocal during the 1980s. He established tens of millions of dollars in greenmail cash before larger corporations like Phillips Petroleum were guided into a formal corporate commitment.

The commitment and direction of the oil companies (c/o Phillips Petroleum) consisted of their merger with Conoco Inc. to become ConocoPhillips. This merger made them the 3rd largest intergraded energy, oil, and gas company in the United States, which also operates in 30 other countries. This is where numerous investors, and corporate raiders positioned themselves to understand a corporate concern within merger/takeover potential activity that ended up on a low end for corporate raiders, and short term investor profits. The consideration of those mergers are similar to ConocoPhillips or even ExxonMobil which for the future American economy can be productive with stronger companies if they don't lose discipline or values as some did before.

As corporations (c/o the oil industry and others) in American business that become older or obsolete it is especially vital to keep up with the changing times. The U.S. Constitution is slightly behind the times of enforcement with various issues of technology, but also in business this becomes the logic of them maintaining business in a corporate capacity of excellence thru lawful disciplines. This becomes important for other Americans reaching their full potential which has benefit's for the entire U.S. economy. Cities Services (c/o Citgo) seem to be one of those companies that needed new resources. The T-Boone Pickens business activity (c/o Mesa Petroleum) was noted as him being an expert on crude oil issues, and the business within corporate raider activity keeping corporate executives conditionally alert.

The hostile takeover business activity of T-Boone Pickens became his constructive and profitable greenmail approach of biding a price for the outstanding shares of a corporation's stock that he held involvement in for decades. Throughout the times of his attempted, or completed hostile takeovers, the American society consisted of some business expansions, and restructuring that was causing businesses to lay-off employees, and evaluate a severe level of foreign competition. The Phillips Petroleum Company during 1984 until about 1987 was another one of T-Boone Pickens strongest targets. His greenmail earnings, and aggressive style of moving at a target company became an occasional public, and private proxy campaign spilling out into public arguments. Before 2002 when Conoco Incorporated merged with Phillips Petroleum (c/o ConocoPhillips), this attracted various corporate raiders, and investors due to the speculation which was becoming the slowdown of T-Boone Pickens apart from then becoming a founder of BP Capital Management.

To understand TLC Beatrice International Holdings Inc., and even Kohlberg Kravis Roberts & Company as it applies to R.J. Reynolds Tobacco Company it is an important observation to know how, and who can restructure a corporation into an economically productive business. The concept of these two companies, and an investment bank is totally different from people who have made business work with certain levels of innovation. These are people like John Johnson (publisher), inventors like Thomas Edison, Henry Ford, Alexander Bell, and George Eastman with a few other innovators of production that created workable businesses in America. Understanding this these people have been good at finding or working with the best people they can find as they keep their own business values of production, and sales prosperous. This also applies to keeping businesspeople working together even if it means working through the good, bad or indifference of government.

As it applies today innovated people such as Lonnie Johnson whom invented a water gun that looks, and operates like a machine gun, these considered products have valuable business potential. These become the consideration of facts that this product during the late 1990s to the 2000s sold millions of low price units is a braking point of popularity. Mark Zuckerberg, whom created the social media computer network Facebook has created a business that is worth billions of dollars, but he want sell to a bigger company. This concept of business means that him, and others will run and expand the company. Steve Jobs was a bit different with Apple Computer Corporation, but guiding a corporation with items like the Macintosh Computer, the iPhone, and other products has taken Apple Inc. into a multi-billion dollar business that one man cannot make, manage, or run by himself. Sometimes this means you need people, and then more people, and even occasional technology. Contrary to this fact one man can leave "A-Point-of-No-Easy-Return" which will last for decades after a vast amount of us living today are long gone, but this established progress must be factual.

Even as Steve Jobs recently passed away at the early age of 57 years old he has made business, and technology expansion visible. Bill Gates with the establishment of Microsoft Corporation, and a diversified group of others created innovated products that are observant by investment bankers, corporations, and occasionally lawyers. This becomes good, and vital resources to help the legal and economic disciplines in lucrative business expansion, and transactions that can cause a repercussion. These are important factors of when business must control issues that consist of extensive laws or legislative government concerns. Understanding this and restructuring a large business operation, their different expertise is not easily compared to long term commitments. These commitments consist of various people working to improve these products, and manufacturing production processes of scientific, mechanical, or publishing resources. This becomes the chance that corporations take with certain corporate raiders as most valued people in these industries make as an effort to be productive.

Throughout the American society of business there is a true value within education, but importantly we also must observe the rank, and file commitments of employees within people working at the company to be a vital asset. This means the time spent within people having hands on experience, and education as willful opportunities in manufacturing, the sales to the general public, various private institutions, and or government becomes an economic necessity. Also included in this equation is the managing of products, services, and employees. Besides R.J. Reynolds with their merged agreements of Nabisco Brands to increase revenue, and their resources Reginald Lewis as CEO and the Chairman of Beatrice International Foods understood certain values. Among these values where corporate law, but he more so needed additional leadership qualities within himself, or someone that could exceed his values of trustworthy business. A valuable Chief Executive Officer, and on occasions the chairman of the board must be able to motivate the employees respectfully for better product division sectors, and increase the output products with values from the corporation. This becomes especially true in restructuring a company just as Reginald Lewis did with one smaller company, but the larger corporate businesses became a conflicting challenge as well.

America has observed a strong restructuring from the company that was founded by George Eastman (c/o Eastman Kodak Company) whom was an inventor and business innovator throughout the early 1900s in the film industry. Contrary to George Eastman holding at least six U.S. Patents under his name, and many more under the Kodak business name, progress existed with stability. Then between the business activities of the Eastman Kodak Company, the "Film" business expanded for decades with a variety of progress at the Kodak Company. These were factors from the "Film" business expanding for decades with the variety of Kodak brands of film, paper, and camera products. This also consisted of some "Chemical" production business issues which today has built the business to provide various chemicals, fibers, and plastics. An improvement to these conditions were led by their own level of corporate raider activity of purchasing certain companies to expand, and to restructure as a corporate business with product demand values.

During 1988 with their former CEO Colby Chandler the Eastman Kodak Company pursued a buyout of Sterling Drugs Co for $5.1 billion dollars, upon which years later they had made secessions to sale-off certain divisions. This became a value which consisted of a partnership of Eastman Kodak/Sterling Winthrop. Some of the product brands involved where Bayer Aspirin, Phillips "Milk of Magnesia", and Lysol. In 1994 Eastman Chemical Company broke away from the Eastman Kodak film business, and became an independent corporation. This included an IPO offered for the Eastman Chemical Company with a listing on the New York Stock Exchange along with the Eastman Kodak Company as two somewhat unrelated corporate businesses. Also this was a business restructuring process with consolidated spin-off agreements of a good, and bad business capacity. Contrary to these business activities certain issues also consisted of the consolidation of business decisions (c/o the buy & sale of business assets) that have achieved economic disciplines in America. Therefore this included some reduced issues of employment opportunities in Rochester, New York, and the concern of their establishment of technology values.

During 2011 some 23 years after the markets, and the economy in the United States changed with Eastman Kodak Company, and the Eastman Chemical Company "division" both had to maintain some level of business prosperity. The managing of a corporate takeover in 1988 of Sterling Drugs Co. consisted of various other business activities which have led Eastman Chemical Company to combine assets productively. This became the productive process which have made the chemical business of Eastman Chemical Company do extremely well with diverse chemical products. The Eastman Chemical Company sense 1988 has increased their value as a company to nearly $7 billion dollars in value. Also the expanded chemical company has consistently been hitting new 52 week highs (above $30 dollars a share) within their 2010/2011 stock price, and dividend payments to shareholders.

The film manufacturing business of Eastman Kodak Company has not done so well as the chemical business, but the film business has held on to a certain level of market presence. During 2011 the Eastman Kodak Company's stock price is selling for about $3.50 a share. This seems to be a process within business where the subsidiary of the parent company values are within the consolidation of decisions by top level management officials, board members, and various shareholders. Another valuable business issue exist within the concern that the Eastman Kodak Company consist of a vast amount of manufacturing facilities in America. The Eastman Chemical Company has 11 factories; 4 in the United States, and 7 in other countries which adds to worldwide business values of economic discipline. The Eastman Kodak's Co. headquarters is in Rochester, New York, and the Eastman Chemical's Co headquarters is in Kingsport, Tennessee. Understanding these issues of American corporate leadership with some values of corporate takeovers, and business transactions various businesses, the people, and government still has a logical money, and tax revenue circulation for survival, but even that weakens in certain regions.

American businesses that have endured hostile, aggressive, or non-hostile corporate takeovers, and or mergers whether being the target company, or being the company that is making an offer to buy a business will usually focus on the issue of a productive outcome, which is vital. One important factor about most corporations in America is that they seldom act as corporate raiders apart from aggressive buyouts, or mergers. This becomes part of their public relations to work along the side of businesses that they will understand future progress with or even as lawful business competitors. Also throughout America this becomes an important issue within professional codes of conduct. Then observing most professionals they hire, their outlook is to be logical citizens as well as beneficial people to the company that consist of citizenship social values with an ambition to survive, and prosper in business.

Considering a few aggressive decisions by large banking institutions in the United States some business issues had to be considered within the productive outcome of a critical buyout, and or merger during a critical economic crisis. This was the case between Citigroup, Wachovia, and Wells Fargo which the U.S. federal government established the Troubled Asset Relief Program (TARP) to rescue the capital liquidity requirements for the survival of certain banks, and businesses. This issue consisted of an aggressive need for the buyout of Wachovia Bank which also heavily included the FDIC Chairwoman Sheila Bair, and the Federal Reserve Chairman Ben Bernanke. The involvement of the federal government became important due to the Wachovia banking establishment's critical condition of financial insecurity during the U.S. economic, and mortgage crisis in the 1st decade of the 2000s.

One of the critical American financial issues within 2008, and 2009 was the economic, and mortgage crisis that affected Wachovia Bank, and the activity at Citigroup "Banking" Incorporated. Before the worse part of this U.S. economic crisis occurred, the Wachovia Bank bought out Golden West Bank whom had more Adjustable Rate Mortgage (ARM) failures than any other bank in the United States. This severely bad corporate buyout by Wachovia took them from being the 4th largest bank in America, to being in worse economic shape than most all other logical bank business establishments. The Countrywide Bank, and Washington Mutual Bank had just suffered similar financial problems, and have went somewhat out of business (c/o receiverships and vital mergers) from a nationwide rate of mortgage failures. This became a tremendous problem creating an economic crisis. Also this led Citigroup's CEO Vikram Pandit, and Wachovia's Chairman Richard Kovacevich to establish an agreement for Citigroup to buy the troubled bank Wachovia.

The merger/buyout agreement between Citigroup, and Wachovia immediately started to seem like a serious problem if you understand Citigroup did not care to take the best management authority on $40 billion dollars of mortgage backed securities that appropriated severe losses. Within days to a week the FDIC, the Treasury Department, and the Federal Reserve determined that this potential merger/buyout would be allowing a troubled bank to purchase another troubled bank with a portfolio of bad loans. Then for Citigroup to complete the buyout of Wachovia, they wanted the U.S. government to provide the following from the FDIC, and the Federal Reserve Bank; and that was to cover $312 billion dollars, but they would only cover $12 billion dollars, and an estimated $4 billion dollars a year over a certain amount of time. Considering this, the FDIC Chairman Sheila Bair with a few others from the Department of Treasury, and the Federal Reserve became extremely questionable about their proposed buyout or merger agreement. This became the point, and time when Wells Fargo decided to make a small alteration to their bid for Wachovia at $7 dollars a share, and that consisted of a buyout without a penny of support from the federal government for this corporate buyout to be approved.

The Wachovia agreement to be bought out by Wells Fargo became appropriate for most involved government officials whom did not want too much of the wrong involvement, and not to put up billions of dollars to support a banking merger or buyout. Actually the SEC regulates, and observes most buyouts or mergers, but they only rarely have the duty or authority to make or recommend who a company should buy, or what company another business should be bought out by. Lately the U.S. government with the FDIC has solicited various qualified banks to buy other troubled banks that have failed. This process is severely confidential until it is affirmed to all bank employees, and then the American general public.

The TARP, and a few other temporary or term lending facility programs were established to lend money at low rates for troubled corporate or banking businesses to secure their liquidity values, and only under severe circumstances for corporate mergers, and or acquisitions. Observing these aggressive corporate merger, and buyout transactions in the banking industry with Bank of America, and their former CEO Ken Lewis, he was severely criticized, and putout of this CEO job for bad decisions with government funded money. This was part of the distinct decisions of their buyout of Countrywide Bank, and more so the attempted buyout of Merrill Lynch after receiving TARP funds. Bank of America did complete the buyout of Countrywide Financial for about $4.1 billion dollars in 2008 as their CEO Angelo Mozilo was pressured from numerous state, and federal government officials about mortgage lending conflicts. This was after Countrywide and their company's tremendous mortgage lending, and mortgage backed security losses were severely evident.

Observing various aggressive, and conditionally vital mergers and buyouts, this is a process that occasionally became a necessity similar to hostile corporate takeovers due to the vast amount of business restructuring work that needed to be done in this corporate atmosphere. Understanding this capacity of work besides how banks are appropriately different in certain mergers, and buyouts than manufacturing, or chemical business processes have more asset values that are at stake for business to be productive. Upon this issue, the logic of business in America has consisted various values that even government needs to be workable for the people, and the American society. Therefore various corporate mergers, buyouts, and management disciplines are of future values that are considered with importance, contrary to corporate raiders. Then the investors, and most business owners including the American system of government have a logical working level of progress.

CHAPTER FOUR
AMERICAN MERGERS IN TRANSITION WITH THE ECONOMY

||||||||||||||||||||||||||||||||||||||||||||||||||||||||||||||||||||||||

The American society of business, and corporate mergers has been a factual conflict within improving the economy in the United States for decades. These various improvements to the U.S. economy occur when corporations restructure successfully, or a vast amount of new business startups are productive within their disciplines of business. Understanding this transaction format of an acquisition also includes businesses that have up's, and down's as it applies to restructuring. Then regaining prosperous business earnings which is the logic of how American businesses restructure has become part of a format to apply the best management with good decisions. This is conditionally based on if the business becomes a vital resource of relevant social values of progress. Corporate mergers "besides" a buyout is one of the major factors of how some businesses, and more so corporations restructure on occasions that can save or improve an existing company, and a region's economy.

A relevant economic and financial transition to observe is factual within the business, and banking crisis during the beginning of the year 2000. Then following this issue within concern for 10 years throughout the United States became a relevant problem for the people suffering through this increasingly bad economy.

Observing this problem the American banking industry, and some large businesses have endured economic, and financial hardships throughout the last few years of the 1ˢᵗ decade of 2000 which has changed American businesses for decades to come. This decade has been tremendous with conflicting values for the American economy, and most corporations that also depend on the American industry of banking, and investment banking. These factors also consist of all issues of American banking that are, and has been associated with "Government Sponsored Enterprises" like Fannie Mae, and Freddie Mac. Then the United States suffered a circumference of financial difficulties with these, and a vast amount of other institutions that could not maintain profitable earnings.

The United States federal government establishment of the Troubled Asset Relief Program (TARP) has provided an estimated 700 institutions, and businesses with a qualified level of financial support of more than $185 billion dollars in the first decade of 2000. This TARP lending was appropriated to help corporate American liquidity exceed critical problems during the recession of the first decade of 2000 with social, and economic disaster concerns that caused grief in America. After the program was activated, and evaluated up to its conclusive support, a certain level of detailed problems occurred in 2008 with 707 different financial institutions having been considered too big to fail. This observation was applied when they received their part of $205 billion dollars of lending from the U.S. government. There also was a remaining $450 billion dollars provided for businesses such as AIG (receiving $70 billion dollars), Citigroup (receiving $20 billion dollars), Bank of America excepting $20 billion dollars, and others in consideration.

Observing the U.S. auto industry, TARP lending provided General Motors, GMAC (now Ally Financial Inc.), Chrysler, and Chrysler Financial all sharing funding in excess of $81 billion dollars from the U.S. federal government whom now have considered them too big to fail. With an enormous amount of American consumers who buy cars, and trucks that were affected by this conflicting economic system the auto industry had to adjust to giving their customer base of Americans economic relief. The format of this relief consisted of them supporting these potential customers with improved vehicle credit, and financing for the purchasing of these products. Then the concept of too big to fail in American business issues became evident within local corporate auto dealerships closing at nearly the same rate as local, or commerce banks. Considering this, these factors of a financial bailout where also considered for a variation of American economic transitional concerns. Therefore the quality, and sales of these vehicles becomes a relevant factor of enormous conditions to the economy throughout America.

Chrysler Corporation is, and has been one of the biggest corporate buyout targets that is not only too big to fail, but also for years it seems that they are too big for anybody else to manage as a productive vehicle manufacturing company in America. The Chrysler Corporation has been a logical producer of automobiles, and a publicly held company up until 2007. Directly before those years of 2001 to 2007 the financial company Cerberus Capital Management, L.P. retained some 81% of the controlling stock of the company for mostly the managing of the pension funds. Two years later, with their CEO Robert Nardelli, and the company whom were still suffering certain economic conflicts within Chrysler Group LLP (c/o corporate restructuring) they did emerge from Chapter 11 reorganization bankruptcy in the month of June 2009.

Soon after, during 2009 the Chrysler Group LLP was then sold to Fiat, an Italian vehicle manufacturing company which this decision had been discussed with certain economic concerns years before. This has been the second automobile partnership within a product extended merger for Chrysler observing their 1998 merger agreement with German based Daimler-Benz AG. Following this merger they became DaimlerChrysler AG that was conflicting to the commitments of American engineering, and conditional retirement issues provided from the former Chrysler CEO Bob Eaton during the 1990s. This merger extension within automobile product business disciplines created DaimlerChrysler Motors Co. LLC seem to still operate as an American company. The noticeable changes usually existed within investment income, product values of production, and or even how layoffs effected employees that had to endure difficulties.

Actually none of these automobile company mergers have made good cars below budget compared to various foreign automakers, but America has its own threshold of financial disciplines. Considering the overall economic conflicts in America this makes a vehicle to be sold to the public conflicting at a price that is tremendously attractive. Upon this considered effort these changes at the Chrysler Corporation have caused a nerve stricken affect to their more than 51,000 employees during 2010. Also over the last 15 years with extensive foreign investors, this occasionally becomes the questionable ability of American labor, and non-labor employees to make this "Chrysler" business workable. This becomes an issue within more ownership, and control of American corporations which becomes the loss of equity opportunities for employment, business prosperity, and investors in America.

These have been issues within the Chrysler Corporation that have suffered various conflicts with vehicle manufacturing, including their business level of production with automobile sales, and appropriate operating standards. Understanding the active concerns of the Chrysler Corporation, and to keep it as a productive part of American business becomes part of a working resource of solutions. These solutions consist of values to manage various automobile product brands. Also its important to clearly observe U.S. government regulation including the people as employees to keep a cost effective level of production that is safe, and vibrant with the best new ideas in technology. These are government, and business disciplines that where slightly considered from the times of their former CEO Lee Iacocca during the 1970s, and 1980s which was slightly behind some of their most interesting automobile products. The effect on the American economy may seem to be tremendous considering during 2008 they sold about 931,402 vehicles apart from an average of 2,200,000 during the previous years. This was slightly a different condition from other business issues of bankruptcy. Therefore this is also slightly indifferent from a vast amount of smaller or less complex corporations that have provided the U.S. economy financial, and economic resources. Then upon this operational format of conditions they have been productive or active with American corporate businesses aiding the American economy, and certain other business constituents.

Corporations in America, as well some worldwide foreign corporate businesses have tried to keep the merger equation of business a logical process of discipline. Observing some of these mergers of even non-hostile buyouts, short term investors occasionally loss. Two American corporations that have endured conflicts to take corporate values from America have been from LG Electronics buying Zenith Corporation, and ISG buying LTV Steel Corporation, Inland Steel Corporation, and Bethlehem Steel Corporation. All of these transactions were quite complex, and indifferent within corporate buyouts which were part of these corporations suffering in strange ways. This occurred before foreign investors (with millions and billions of dollars) began making a controlling purchase of the stock in these companies. Understanding this concern some foreign investors, and businesses are continuing to make billions of dollars in business. This observation even applies with U.S. government bonds that are offered as U.S. Treasury investments which some American business values are becoming non-competitive to foreign business. Therefore these types of business issues, and purchases will continue until the legal discipline of U.S. business has lawful equity, "distinctively within the U.S. Constitution" being argued with logical fairness for all citizens possible.

Zenith Corporation after their start in 1923 invented, produced, and sold the first portable radio, and one of the first automobile push button radio systems at a very large capacity rate of sales throughout the United States. During this time all automobiles sold to consumers where manufactured with radios purchased from companies such as Zenith Corporation. Then later, their level of production continued with various advancements in televisions including the expanded concept of remote control television sets for numerous decades. These are levels of corporate progress which sometimes includes the values of high labor cost that must be controlled just like most lower, and upper management business values. This also included Civil

Defense (Fire & Police communication equipment), and United States Department of Defense communications equipment, which is part of defending, and supporting America. Conditionally these were the years of Motorola, and Zenith Corporation being fierce competitors throughout a complex market that span thru every state in America.

During the 1970s, and more so the 1980s Zenith Corporation, and other American electronic manufacturing businesses where being matched by Japanese companies, and their intense factories of extensive production. These foreign competitors, and businesses had lower overhead cost, and provided more inventory for retail stores which helped keep the lower cost within products being sold to American consumers inexpensive. Observing the troubles at Zenith Corporation they decided to put themselves into a technology merger with LG Electronics selling them 5% of the Zenith Corporation in the early 1990s. By 1999 Zenith Corporation filed for bankruptcy which gave LG Electronics a Korean company opportunity to increase their holdings of stock in the Zenith Corporation to well over 50%. This was an aggressive takeover that was slightly just outside of a corporate hostile takeover, accept for the American discipline of Zenith Corporation's technology that held vital presence.

Zenith Corporation being an important defense contractor similar to other American corporations like LTV Steel Corporation, Inland Steel Company, and Bethlehem Steel Corporation at one time means that America, and the U.S. government has loss certain values of control. This becomes the observation of U.S. defense technology values that are important to various resources of business, and secured U.S. government technology. LG Electronics being a Korean company, and their purchase of the Zenith Corporation has conflicts that started before the U.S. and Korean War during the 1950s. Most of these conflicts consisted of issues within how people, government, and their relationships with developing defense, and civilian products were established, and protected. This sense of logical protection is part of defense for American solders that were injured or killed in the Korean War, and years later the Vietnam War including other war conflicts with defense technology that becomes a discussion of relevant U.S. government concerns.

These oriental countries with different conditions of law are a conflict of interest occasionally in America that do not apply or compare to various activities in business that had to be controlled by the laws of the U.S. Constitution. Observing this U.S. Constitutional issue means the logic within laws must hold relevance within various lawful operations of how companies maintain a U.S. domestic presence. This becomes the importance of the United States, and the government (c/o the Legislature & the Judiciary) which have observation of the United States Constitution being amended or argued in the Supreme Court. This observation is important to adjust any unfairness, or laws from another country. These are the type of laws, and legal conflicts that destroys the integrity of the American society of people, employees, businesses, corporations, and or other logical business investments, and social concerns.

Contrary to the U.S. Constitution, or International laws during the late 1950s certain levels of war time production provided the Bethlehem Steel Corporation economic, and financial values to get things done. This became the increased values to compensate building one of the newest, and most innovated steel mills in America on the shores of Northwest Indiana's Burns Harbor. Observing the valuable American concern of technology just as the Zenith Corporation was being taken control of by LG Electronics, a few years later Bethlehem Steel Corporation was becoming the target of "Foreign Corporate Raider-Ship" concerns. This was the point of American industry where conflicting accidents, and cost effective measures exceeded their earnings over the years, but sometimes this was due to high corporate taxes. Also certain other economic conflicts occurred from foreign competition against a weaker American workforce that did not maintain long-term corporate values. International Steel Group (ISG) with their founder Wilber Ross whom then agreed to a merger/buyout acquisition with Mittal Steel eliminating most U.S. ownership became the weakest point for American investors, and various American investment concerns.

Bethlehem Steel Corporation manufactured steel used in certain parts of the Golden Gate Bridges (c/o California), various U.S. Defense Department battle ships for war, and other American made structures upon this company being taken control of by Lakshmi Mittal whom is from India. Considering small American investors, and some issues of American businesspeople this loss of U.S. manufacturing to foreign control, and interest became a slight concern to most people involved. Therefore this included citizens, government, and the logical observation of the American steel industry to become more progressive.

The Bethlehem Steel Corporation before the transaction, had served various resources of U.S. defense, and diversified industries. This was an issue that sometimes can have U.S. Constitutional law concerns, but America has lately been a country that has had serious illegal immigration, and foreign relation problems. Also throughout the United States certain foreign people have been provided opportunities until factual debates became relevant to the government, and most citizens including businesses in the American general public. Other issues from the United States government came into effect less than a few years after the 2001 acquisition which restricted Mittal Steel from certain defense contract's. This was a factor from the Bethlehem Steel Corporation losing its financial, and economic discipline that applies to certain government, and industry standards in America. Therefore they were forced to file bankruptcy in 2001 which seem to occur after a few fatal accidents as well with the likes of terrorism or severe issues of negligence that should have been workable, but did not go right.

The concept and acquisition by Mittal Steel and ISG consisted of (3) American steel companies; which were Inland Steel Company, Bethlehem Steel Corporation, and the LTV Steel Corporation. These three businesses created value, high ratings of production, and liquidity that where compounded with a large quantity of American land, household concerns, and business assets. This mostly existed between Indiana, Illinois, Texas, Ohio, Pennsylvania, and a few other states. Observing the LTV Corporation before their bankruptcy and aggressive takeover that was packaged with these other corporate businesses, they had become a company of strong resources. The LTV Corporation with their CEO/Chairman Raymond Hay engaged in the business of Aerospace/Defense, Energy related products, the Meat & Food industry, and their production of Steel. During 1983 their AM General, and Sierra Research business concept of discipline manufactured the 1st set of Hummer military vehicles, and by 2004 this product had become a civilian vehicle sold to the American general public. From there by 1985 they had increased production to the rate of 55,000 vehicles for delivery to the U.S. military for $1.2 billion dollars. They also served a contract with the U.S. Air Force for B-B1 bombers. Also for $1.2 billion dollars another manufacturing process at LTV Corporation consisted of production at various times of manufacturing 3,000 rockets a month in their Multiple Launch Rocket system program. During 1984 other business activity consisted of a merger with Republic Steel Corporation resulting in LTV becoming the second largest steel manufacturing company in America behind U.S. Steel Corporation.

AM General acquired various military vehicle contracts (c/o the Humvee/Hummer) from the U.S. Department of Defense (contrary to LTV) which is a valued American business headquartered in South Bend, Indiana. This included an AM General assembly plant in nearby Mishawaka, Indiana. These issues increased after LTV Corporation was dissolved. The U.S. government did outline the qualifications of U.S. Defense contractors especially as it applies within protecting American national security. Contrary to LTV Corporation's short time within ownership of AM General when the LTV Corporation bought them from the American Motors Corporation, these were expandable business issues. On the other side of concern, the U.S. government followed up with the managing of defense, and technology spending on American products of importance. These activities with federal issues of law for U.S. Defense contract procurements are regulated by laws within the Berry Amendment that requires the Department of Defense (DOD) to give preference to U.S. domestically produced or manufactured American products. Some of these products range from food, clothing, fabrics, and specialty metals.

Observing metals in the steel industry lately, and the increasing concept of various computer programs, these products have been added to this U.S. industry concern of business with the U.S. federal government. These are issues that apply to the U.S. government's Federal Procurement Policy Act upon which these become values within the authority of the Secretary of Defense. This important issue has been considered as these products were developed for certain U.S. Defense Department activities, and the various branches of the U.S. military and some international military concerns. Observing the merger acquisitions surrounding AM General such as within the buyout acquisitions by ISG, and ArcelorMittal Steel national security became conflicting to the issues within India, the Middle East, and certain conditions throughout Europe. Understanding this level of U.S. National Security the Berry Amendment was observed along with the U.S. Federal Acquisition Regulation program to ensure security. This legal factor within amendments is to regulate the private sector firms that are incorporated into government solicitation, and the conflicts offered within their professional, and business levels of reference that become closely monitored issues.

The U.S. Congress originally passed certain domestic source restrictions as part of the 1941 Fifth Supplemental DOD Appropriations Act to protect America's domestic industrial base during times of war. The U.S. Defense Federal Acquisition Regulation Supplement (DFARS) Act with a program which was amended to include exceptions for the acquisition of food, specialty metals, and a consolidation of hand or measuring tools was vital to maintain confidential products that apply to the U.S. Defense Department. This issue during 2009 became the Kissel Amendment (c/o U.S. Rep. Larry Kissel) which was part of the American Recovery and Reinvestment Act. The logic of this was important within making U.S. Homeland Security procurement contracted products a priority requirement to be manufactured in the United States. These are products that are needed to support various U.S. contingency operations. Operating disciplines that are important to the U.S. issues of defense, and civil service matters includes various concerns of the Coast Guard, or other military agency activities. This becomes the contingency values of when the use of other-then-competitive procedures is based on an unusual and compelling urgency with inventory, and activities which can consist of a rapid response.

Most times government, and private industry includes contingent U.S. national security support values that become important as a bipartisan concern of protecting the overall American society. This regulation (c/o 1973) goes as far as to outline that specialty metals incorporated in products delivered under DOD contracts to be melted in the United States or a "qualified country". Specialty metals include certain steel, titanium, zirconium, and other alloys that are important to the DOD. Therefore the AM General LLC, and their parent company the "Renco Group, Inc" are businesses that provide services that the U.S. Defense Department understands as appropriate with qualifications.

As a vast amount of people in the Midwest observed various concerns in steel mill operations, and their corporate business values during the 1970s up to the 1990s the people, and industry occasionally suffered. Considering the Inland Steel Company founder Philip Block & Family's business, there was no exception to this working process, and industry within good, and bad times. This was his observation to the steel industry in the early 1900s within his financing, and restructuring of a suffering steel company which took time, and effort to achieve progress. This vital effort which became Inland Steel, the company held its progress for over 80 years until a buyout and merger with ISG and Mittal. This was evident within independent companies similar to Inland Steel Company with its presents located next to U.S. Steel Corporation's Gary Works plant that also endured similar concerns, but they survived as a U.S. business operation worldwide.

The Inland Steel Company endured a serious amount of setbacks within problems during the 1980s, and decided to form a joint venture to improve their earnings, and production of steel products. Inland Steel's joint venture was established with Nippon Steel; a Tokyo, Japan steel company that is ranked presently (c/o 2011) as the 4th largest in steel production volume throughout the world. After various additional struggles, the Inland Steel company had a concern to be acquired, and this led to the Ispact International agreement within a corporate business buyout. A few years later Inland Steel's assets (c/o East Chicago, Indiana & Chicago, IL) became part of ArcelorMittal to create one of the largest steel companies in the world which later included a $40 billion acquisition of a steel company in Europe. The East Chicago, IN. former Inland Steel plant, and now ArcelorMittal Steel operation is located on the "Indiana Harbor and Ship Canal" which in recent years is one of the (45th) busiest "harbors in America". This Indiana Harbor has been known to handle over 13 million short tons of steel annually, and hundreds of thousands of foreign trade products being transported throughout Lake Michigan, and Canada.

Understanding the Midwest of the United States within U.S. Defense contractors the transition of Amoco Oil Company being bought out by British Petroleum plc (BP) that shifted a percentage of financial values to London, England was conflicting to American values, and some tax revenue concerns. Besides gas, oil, and other chemical products Amoco Oil Corporation manufactured trinitrotoluene (TNT) for 120mm mortar bombs, and other large tonnage capacity explosives. In World War II Standard Oil (c/o Amoco) supplied aviation, land gasoline for military vehicles, and various fuels to the Allied forces. They improved various chemical divisions within business from a merger of Pan American Chemicals Company, and the Indoil Chemical Company. After the buyout, British Petroleum also acquired these U.S. defense contracts worth billions of dollars, and other conditional asset management concerns. During 2007, and 2008 the BP plc contracts with the United States government were worth more than $1.7 billion dollars annually. It's appropriate that BP and England is an ally to the United States, but we as Americans must still try to maintain the businesses that the American society, and people have provided so many sacrifices to establish.

A vast amount of American mergers with enormous assets in transition with the U.S. economy has outlined a discipline for business, and economic restructuring of prosperity in most concerns throughout the United States. This is valued within the American society of business, and government that must restructure its values within small businesses growing into larger businesses that are productive. Another important detail is the offer provided to Americans to stand on their Constitutional rights, and values within business startup's, and expansion. Then we look at Japan, China, India, and on occasions Mexico as we believe in fair international rules of law, and business, but our American rights that all Americans are born to value is within the outlined opportunities that are similar to prosperous companies. These are companies such as Walmart, Johnson's Publishing Company, Dell Computer Corp, MTV, BET, certain internet companies, and even Microsoft Corporation. These companies, and businesses that where started or that expanded over the "last 25 years or more" were part of hard work with people using their Constitutional rights of prosperity to advance in business. Without these values within American laws the United States would be slipping into worse shape than the present 2010 economy, and social conflicts that we recognize in other countries that have little understanding of domestic tranquility.

As American's continue to move ahead with "hopefully" maintaining a prosperous economy, especially when some companies are needing a merger or buyout concern, and others don't, the people will look up too these businesses for values of opportunities. This occurs due to business debt which leads to social problems, and conflicts. The values within opportunities is an important part of business, and corporate conditions just like colleges, and universities outline studies that these economic conditions consist of for industry. Contrary to new expanded businesses that have did fairly well, a vast amount of businesses have accumulated severe debt which have affected various conditions of social conflicts that negatively affect society. While General Electric Corporation was creating good earnings buying out other corporations, and improving various products, similar corporate concerns such as at Enron Corporation, and some other businesspeople severely instigated, and committed tremendous levels of fraud against America. This caused a problem that has been pushing American values full speed backwards.

WorldCom Corporation, and Enron Corporation have created so much debt, and damage it will take years or decades for most people who were invested in these companies, and loss to restructure. People close to the Enron Corporation considering their headquarters in Texas that loss dearly, it also effected other people in certain regions of America. An enormous amount of accounting irregularities occurred within their business activities coming from Arthur Andersen Accounting which lead the U.S. Congress, and government to establish the Serbanes-Okley Act . The observation of this legislature that became law was important to regulate accounting practices for certain improved business issues of lawful disciplines within business accounting. This was vital within the economic capacity of damage that they even caused to the State of California. The CEO's of Enron Ken Lay, and Jeff Skilling's activities at the Enron Corporation was valued with revenue, and asset values exceeding $120 billion dollars before bankruptcy, and massive financial fraud. Their "Energy Trading" fraud capacity of damage cost the State of California over $40 billion dollars in electrical blackouts became a manipulated level of fraud through financial, and energy transactions of conflict.

Enron Corporation was one of many billion dollar issues of fraud with various contractors to hedge or trade energy services, but WorldCom (c/o MCI) had communication issues of business in almost all parts of America, and some conditions of business throughout the world within developed countries. Enron Corporation established their business expansion with only two corporate merger/buyout acquisitions which gave them control of a regional utility market within Portland General Electric. Although Enron Corporation also did business in other parts of the world, issues of a communication company similar to WorldCom Corporation with MCI consisted of more service business matters. WorldCom Corporation's business disciplines consisted of the long distance telephone market, and industry that was about to exceed the business activity at American Telephone & Telegraph (AT&T) during the WorldCom extensive business expansion within anti-trust issues, and fraud. MCI was active in the original breakup of the AT&T monopoly within corporate mergers, and or buyouts, and therefore them, and other businesses spun out of control. This problem included at least $50 billion dollars of financial leverage conditions of bank lending cash that was another economic conflict in the American economy.

The WorldCom Corporation achieved business expansion from numerous corporate or business buyouts, and mergers. Observing the companies that were merged or bought out by WorldCom were the Advanced Communications Corporation in 1992, Metromedia Communication Corporation in 1993, also Resurgens Communications Group in 1993, IDB Communications Group, Inc in 1994, Williams Technology Group Inc in 1995, and MFS Communications Company during 1996. This was an excessive Junk Bond market process that removed a vast amount of companies from their individual level of active business. Contrary to their active business discipline some business people, owners, and investors may have welcomed the buyout issue of value which was paid for to gain a controlling ownership of these target buyout companies. Therefore this was a dot-com bubble, and a junk bond market out of control with WorldCom leading other businesses with conflicting control.

Some issues within the theory of a Junk Bond, and merger/ buyout market being out of control which completely describes MCI WorldCom, and a few other companies were part of business "restructuring, and expansion". Before WorldCom's acquisition of MFS Communications Company, this market issue included UUNET Technologies, Inc whom had been acquired by MFS Communications Company a short time before the merger with WorldCom Corporation. The WorldCom Corp with Bernard Ebbers bought out CompuServe from its parent company H&R Block during February of 1989. This was a diversified computer products transaction considering the complex purchase with acquisition agreements. Therefore WorldCom retained the CompuServe Network Services Division, and sold the online services to America Online (AOL), and in exchange they received AOL's network division of ANS.

Between 1997 WorldCom and MCI worked together to agree to a merger worth $37 billion dollars to become "MCI" WorldCom" which was considered one of the largest mergers in U.S. history. Following that in 1999 within the month of October, the Sprint Corporation, and MCI WorldCom announced a $129 billion dollar merger between these two (2) companies. These agreements ultimately would have made the largest corporate merger in U.S. history, and would have put these combined companies ahead of AT&T as the largest communications company in America, and the world. This deal did not go thru because of disagreements concerning international Anti-Trust law concerns with regulators conditionally between the United States, and Europe. Considering this the U.S. Department of Justice would not approve the acquisition.

Considering the 1990s a vast amount of WorldCom corporate merger and buyout activity occurred for years, but during July of 2002 WorldCom Corporation filed for Chapter 11 bankruptcy protection. This was the largest bankruptcy filing in U.S. history until Lehman Brothers, and Washington Mutual filed for bankruptcy which occurred during September of 2008. These became indicators of concern which was during the height of the U.S. mortgage banking crisis. Within the mist of this economic conflict, Bernard Ebbers the WorldCom CEO had reneged on hundreds of millions of dollars of margin (call) stock transactions which most of this activity included his ownership of WorldCom stock.

To compare Comcast, Verizon, or AT&T to this corporate issue of WorldCom's intentional condition of greed, and a severe lack of business discipline various government, and management values where ignored. This severe problem lead to a communication industry in America becoming problematic within corporate mergers, and or more so with Constitutional law concerns. Then therefore this outlined another harmful conflict that included small companies which were the subjects of violations within various U.S. Anti-Trust laws which became part of an overall loss within merged businesses gone bad.

Various issues of U.S. Anti-Trust law violations, and certain corporate business concerns becomes a losing factor to the importance of small productive, or expanding businesses in America when laws are ignored. The U.S. Attorney Alberto Gonzales with his government Division of Anti-Trust did not take appropriate awareness of this problem until billions of dollars had been misguided within corporate ignorance, and fraudulent delight. These factors of fraudulent business in various markets hurt the American society of business, and the true prosperity offered in the U.S. Constitution within small businesses gaining logical prosperity. Considering these issues a vast amount of corporate mergers and buyouts during the 1990s became part of a losing American market for diversified business failures. This is "not" always the result of normal reactions, but with certain businesses involved in multi-billion dollar issues of fraud, and even negligence various parts of the American economy were negatively affected. These conflicts with the BP Companies two accidents, the tragic effects of Enron, and WorldCom business purchases were all an equation of failure with a repercussion effect. This included crimes, some negligence, and issues of fraud upon which the mortgage crisis with hundreds of banks failing are just a few transactions leading to a negative U.S. economy. These negative factors were bad for their businesses, and affected other smaller businesses, and markets in a diversified array of harmful ways.

Other businesses have gave America a positive transition observing Eastman Chemical Company, Microsoft Corp, Apple Computer Co, Walmart, U.S. Steel Corp, and General Electric Corp to name a few that have made progress. The automobile industry in America is restructuring with an increased level of activity from Ford Motor Company, and General Motors Corporation. Contrary to these auto industry factors Chrysler Corp is still struggling with interesting American made cars and trucks, but their economic values will seem to consist of additional work with good decisions from management, and labor unions. This leaves us as Americans with the effort to continue the need within issues of employment to improve, and even be helpful to the American people becoming involved productively as small business owners that expand. Therefore we must work hard at being better managers of business without the loss of important disciplines of labor, government, and a well-developed American society.

CHAPTER FIVE

THE SEC AND THE PROTECTION OF U.S. CORPORATE REAL ASSETS

||||||||||||||||||||||||||||||||||||||||||||||||||||||||||||||||

The United States Securities and Exchange Commission (SEC) has a duty to enforce the rules, regulation, and laws within assets that are offered as investments throughout the American society of business. This becomes the important format to protect American investors and their assets that become vital as it applies to logical, and or long term security. Both short term, and long term investments that help manage, and expand business or personal finances are some of the most vital ways in America to manage, and create levels of wealth. Therefore with at least $5 to $8 trillion dollars of corporate American assets to invest in, there is an enormous amount of small, and large investment concerns for the SEC to protect. Then these investors with government regulation, and knowledgeable people can make an effort of working in diversified businesses, professional businesses, and throughout the U.S. system of government.

One of the few large business owners of America whom made good with some bad investments that leveled off losses with other business issues of progress was Ted Turner. His ownership values have went from advertisement, to professional sports, and cable television media holdings that over the decades have created positive, and steady economic disciplines of growth. From this, the business transactions with procedures of Ted Turner whom created TNT, and CNN which consisted of expanded cable television movies, and news networks has been a positive resource in America. Observing compliance with the SEC, the FCC, and even the National Baseball League (NBL) his ownership within the Atlanta Braves, the Hulks, and others with televised broadcast conditions have become a level of logical business progress. This occurred throughout the years of the 1970s to the present day of 2012. This becomes important to the good, and bad investments of corporate American activity which includes the merger, and or buyout process so that laws, and values within transactions are pursued fairly within the rules of Constitutional law, and most market transactions.

Considering cash money, and various other items are vital assets when American businesses consider mergers, buyouts, or investments concerning American companies the equipment, and property are a necessity to be workable upon any establishing, or restructuring of business. Also the products as inventory that are manufactured is part of the real assets that make money for most all logical businesses. Observing these issues of asset investments which are part of the logical reason why the Securities Act of 1933 was established, became the disciplines of registration of securities with antifraud provisions. These antifraud provisions prohibit false representation of a corporation, or most business assets, and any activities by way of lawful disclosures. Also, and more importantly the registration of securities prior to public sale, and adequate "Disclosures" of pertinent financial and other data is provided in a "Prospectus". The lawful SEC requirement within the prospectus is to permit an informed analysis to potential investors which is a vital factor within investing their life savings, and or a percentage of income earnings. Therefore even if the inventory of a business has become nonexistent the land, buildings, and other assets usually hold value in America that is vital to be recognized.

Contrary to the mortgage economic crisis of 2008, and 2009 a junk bond market (c/o Enron & WorldCom) before the year of 2000 became fraudulent, and out of control. Bernard Ebbers and WorldCom used the merger/buyout process within the financial markets extensively to expand various business assets, and to monopolize control in the U.S. Communications market. Apart from the billions of dollars, and the 10s of thousands of employees removed from these 2 companies with their losses, they also left America with billions of dollars of idol real estate, and debt. This business disaster consisted of various assets which were seized by the U.S. government, and then taken control of by individual businesspeople familiar with those corporate American business assets. Some assets were also part of their foreign investments that are slightly controlled by foreign government concerns. Considering the level of court proceedings, and various issues of prosecution most of these assets are now supervised by the U.S. federal government until all matters have been considered through the state, and federal courts for resolution.

The United States Federal Trade Commission, and then the U.S. Securities and Exchange Commission shared the enforcement of securities, and investment laws from 1933 up until around 1935 when the SEC was becoming a productively ran government enforcement operation. The Securities and Exchange Commission was established as an agency in 1934. It was created from the Securities Exchange Act which consisted of the Public Utility Holding Company Act of 1935, the Trust Indenture Act of 1939, and the Investment Advisors Act of 1940. In 1975 the Securities Act Amendments directed the SEC to facilitate the National Market System for clearance, and settlement of securities transactions. Also this same amendment established the Municipal Securities Rule Making Board whose rules are subject to SEC approval. Observing these factors, most utility companies have did well excluding Enron Corporation, but the loss of U.S. tax revenue in various regions caused Municipal Bond ratings to tremendously be downgraded.

During the Ronald Reagan U.S. presidential administration various business owners with investments made prosperous gains that helped American businesses expand. Observing him as a former governor of California, and then the president of the United States the American society became progressive with expansions and this included keeping labor unions guided with Constitutional values.

He also at that time endured the Air Traffic Controller unions strike which was a delicate situation. Considering the former U.S. President Ronald Reagan whom made a bulk of his wealth from acting in movies, this industry concern has suffered as well. This is an industry that must make good decisions about how good the actors are, and the interest of a movie that people will pay to see. Understanding the format of business owners within individuals like Ted Turner who took financial, and investment interest in buying the Metro-Goldwyn-Mayer (MGM) studios, he offered cable television viewers old classic movies they appreciated. This was a struggling business with certain bankruptcy issues were new ideas including people was helpful. Therefore this becomes an advancement within the changing times of business that have workable values.

The concept of various movies are usually long term assets that make additional money long after most actors with royalties are deceased or when they are consolidated with the cost of living. Contrary to the large transactions of General Electric Corp with NBC, and Ted Turner with MGM throughout Ronald Reagan's tenure as Governor of California apart from his presidency, America and California was starting to recognize these corporate or business assets for long term values. This included the lower levels of production that where important for business assets, and occasionally liquidity to expand. Observing this the American movie making industry has a value within assets, and the ownership of exclusive legal rights to films, and music recordings. These exclusive rights are similar to when MGM studios was bought by Ted Turner which he retained the rights to most all of their established film, and television library which they had accumulated over past decades. This also included the Warner Brothers business process of handling this format of entertainment distribution.

Following the 1990s these conditions of investment security, and financial protection have taken on various hard times due to a percentage of large businesses involved in fraud or failing in competition to foreign business. Sometimes an American business person has to consider; is the state and U.S. federal Constitution being violated in this format of competitive business. Then contrary to the laws some large companies lose economic stability or the ability to upgrade a manufacturing facility. These conflicts with technology advancements occasionally leave abandon manufacturing, and industrial plants in various locations throughout certain regions in the United States. These are conflicting resources of property asset values of concern which has become part of the American way of business whether the times are good, or bad.

America has one of the largest capacities of abandon factories, and buildings in the world. Besides certain corporate buyouts and transactions to sell business subsidiaries there is a tremendous difference in business facilities throughout companies like U.S. Steel Corporation, AT&T Corporation, Intel Corporation, and Microsoft Corporation. These newer businesses (c/o Microsoft Corp, Intel Corp, and a few others) have expanded with wealth, and asset property expansion values which consist of very few idol properties. Considering the older companies (c/o U.S. Steel, AT&T, Ford Motor Co & General Motors Corp) they are continuously going through restructuring, and these transactions are sometimes an evaluation to offset their profits. Therefore with the sale of their business real estate or subsidiary within concerns of adding to their profits, this usually consist of properties they consider as unworkable.

How older businesses have problems within their earnings is one important factor of protecting assets, but various small investors involved in local businesses to expand have been victimized more then they can afford to expand or even operate normally. Too many victims in small business expansions have kept Americans from making investments in real estate, or being productive within buying industrial properties. These are occasionally issues that were factored from a severely damaged regional, and nationwide economy which lately has consisted of a certain amount of bad corporate mergers, and buyout issues that did not work. The U.S. economy has also suffered in other ways, but bad transactions that did not produce logical values, or that consist of too much fraud with criminal conflicts has pushed America backwards with foreign competition gaining economic values. This also includes the property which some foreign investors or businesspeople buy, and control on American soil. Understanding these real assets of importance, and income earnings in America from various conflicting business values has caused a loss of revenue problems to government. Additionally this has also caused an increase in unemployment with idol business properties, and even government facilities that may be next in line to be idol.

Every sense the tenures of Richard Breeden (1989 to 1993), and Arthur Levitt (1993 to 2001) during their work as Chairman's of the Securities and Exchange Commission, the American society of small investors whom own businesses have suffered in various ways. Richard Breeden helped various parts of America recognize the need to eliminate abusive tax shelters throughout Americas resource of active, and more so abandon properties. These properties where part of American real estate eye sores, but this has gotten bad again with the American mortgage crisis which became another strong asset with severe repercussions. This problem made various Americans incapable of financial advancements to upgrade their financial wealth, and real estate properties throughout America. Richard Breeden has also been considered an advisor to the troubled WorldCom Corporation, but this may have been part of a helpful resource to save the liquidity of a failing large American corporation. WorldCom Corporation was a severe part of the regulatory discipline of the Federal Communication Commission (FCC) which they had to comply with throughout their format of business. Considering this factor of the American system of investors whom can achieve wealth (c/o mergers, and transactions) the connection between those people making gains financially thru investors has a need to be observed to keep prosperous business growth.

During 2005 Arthur Levitt as the SEC Chairman was appointed within the President Bill Clinton administration whom also served in the 2nd George Bush administration, reviewed a prosperous looking level of the financial markets with extensive movements, and gains. These economic gains were tremendous with the Dow Jones Average going above 9,000 to 10,000 until the discovery of problems at Ameritech Corp, Enron Corp, and the WorldCom Corporation. These corporations with strong investment interest in their company and others offered additional economic severe conflicts to the American economy.

Arthur Levitt also became active, and helpful to the American International Group (AIG) which outlines certain individuals from government that are closely connected to business, but the American small independent businesses still suffered. Observing the WorldCom Corp after the tenure of Arthur Levitt as Chairman of the SEC the United States also was devastated by the mortgage crisis which also included severe layoffs in other industries such as banking. Small American business owners suffer when these conditions of banking, insurance, and mortgage legal disciplines are not stable, and lawfully helpful to business, or even private life. Considering all of these issues an enormous amount of Middle Eastern businesses in America expanded throughout the ownership of gas stations with some franchised businesses that provided conflicts through various major oil companies. This problem also shifted a money circulation from America to the Middle East, and sometimes into the hands of international terrorism.

Within observing Arthur Levitt, and his involvement within American International Group which is one of the largest American insurance companies in the United States, him and Richard Breeden became a pivotal resource. This became conflicting within these various issues, and factors between the U.S. government, William Donaldson, and Chris Cox upon which these economic values of corporate businesses affected small expanding business operations. The observation of this becomes an issue with business losses that where considered within the financial bailout of too big to fail businesses. All of these business, and government values required severe corrections that needed to be completely in order as millions of American's make an effort to restructure from the damage of AIG, and others.

One of the strongest business conflicts that occurred in the United States sense the early 1990s has been the increase of international investments that occasionally included international terrorism. The 2 attacks on the New York World Trade Center's (c/o 1993 & 2001), and the attacks on the U.S. Department of Defense (at the Pentagon-

DOD) was partly a vital example of well-funded terrorist plots. These terrorist levels of destruction were a problem that the U.S. government, and Corporate America failed to prevent in any form, fashion, or way. This is where America became complacent within their duties throughout business, and more so government with corporate buyouts, and the harm applied to the small companies with values of revenue. These issues of American's being victimized by pushing financial matters in the wrong direction left people between the Middle East, and far South America to become a controlling factor in American business, and the currency.

Observing the advisement of National Security advisor Condoleezza Rice to President George Bush, the activities of the U.S. government inherited a national security, and defense problem that would affect America for years to come. The Pentagon-DOD damage, the two World Trade Center's buildings, the four commercial airplanes that were destroyed (c/o victimized people) observed in the 9-11 Report was a tremendous loss of assets. These American assets were valued in the billions of dollars, and with other concerns this increased to more than a trillion dollars. Besides the 9-11 Report of terrorism, these attacks also consisted of the Pentagon having also suffered from a few small shooting incidents. Observing this conflict, the American economy has been occasionally more supportive of these same naturalized, or nationalized citizens as they buy guns, and bomb making materials. Also on occasions the SEC has taken the side of certain politicians, and some businesspeople that ignored or diverted these various important details until it was too late for some Americans to survive.

Another resource of vital U.S. assets with government, and corporate details of economic disciplines consisting of problems is the American infrastructure, national security, and various business issues. A vast amount of these issues with good, and more so bad foreign relations in business prevented a certain amount of the best upgrades to the infrastructure due to language, or educational differences, defamation, and U.S. Anti-Trust law conflicts. Then U.S. corporate and business control by foreign people have made U.S. National Security very expensive at the state, and federal level of government. This is observed where tax revenue has decreased, and an American money circulation has been provided to other countries. Therefore how we apply, and argue the vital concerns of the U.S. Constitution various American businesspeople whom were victims of defamation, and various U.S. Anti-Trust laws became vitally important similar to victims, and acts of terrorism. These conditions have created a level of suffering that caused failure within logical progress in America's well established assets.

Considering bad government that is "not for the people" a certain amount of American government has failed to manage domestic tranquility, and prosperity with corporate, and individual citizen assets having suffered in various ways. Contrary to bad corporate buyouts, and or terrorist damage, the prevention cost of terrorism have kept the cost of living in America a bit higher for most government officials, and the people to be productive. Actually between the mid-1990s, and up to 2007 the banks, and government may have provided too much for the people by providing them mortgages that they could not afford. These factual problems caused America to have too much excess inventory in real estate properties, and during the financial slow down various construction businesses suffered with a historical amount of consumer victims of foreclosure.

As other damages apply when the SEC provides complacent enforcement activities which has slipped in many ways, this has cost everyday citizens their life savings. One critical factor was within mortgage backed securities that were offered at various investment banks with loans that originated in a vast amount of commerce or local banks whom took severe losses as well. This became the concern of Ben Bernanke the Chairman of the U.S. Federal Reserve Bank whom took observation that these mistakes needed fixing. Also this became a conflict in a workable banking industry, but Ben Bernanke, and others realized that government needed to restructure this entire industry problem. The format of this problem with a solution was different from the Great Depression, and this included his decision with the approval from the administration of the President, and Congress to loan more money to these institutional banking establishments. Along with additional regulation this was vital to rescue there liquidity operating values as Bank Holding Company requirements. Therefore in some sense when it came to fraudulent business, certain loans, and various social activities with government decisions became vital. In all logic these decisions between the President, the Congress, the FDIC, the Treasure Dept., the SEC, and the Federal Reserve Bank were not part of a solution until economic disaster had become severe.

Some issues at the SEC where considered for enforcement after financial damage was done. This consist of when the SEC regulators had only considered certain businesses, and people (c/o mergers or buyout transactions) a minor problem. Then the SEC officials were informed by investors and market indicators that the invested income earnings that were not enough to go around as productive returns on their money invested had not been invested properly. This became a time in America when the most important business people in various industries whom should have said "NO", bid not say No, and it has caused a tremendous economic disaster. Even the word "YES" is vitally important as it applies to the right decisions in the American society, and the world we live in, but this even more so means that productive professional evaluations are vital.

Adding to various economic conflict's consisted of Bernard Madoff's ponzi factor of fraud with losses of $18 billion dollars, and Bernard Ebbers at WorldCom Corporation with nearly $100 billion dollars of corporate and investment losses, the American economy was headed for trouble. Also Kenneth Lay at Enron Corporation losing in access of $11 billion dollars, which included in access of over $40 billion dollars in public utility conditions of fraud, and other people and businesses with losses in the millions of dollars, the concept of liquidity with debt in America was increasing. Even such losses as Amoco becoming BP, Zenith becoming LG, and others like Maytag whom have resource contributory losses to the American money circulation, this has led the American society to its complex need of restructuring the economy. Upon observing the Maytag Company being bought out by Whirlpool Corp, and then moving certain Whirlpool Corp manufacturing units to Mexico have consisted of some conditional economic factors within losses. Then the American society within assets of income earning opportunities suffered losses as well.

A vast amount of conflicts pertaining American business, and government assets required extensive protection during the first decade of the year 2000. This was recognized with the lawful observation, and disclosers of various corporate activities which gave government, some concerning issues, and businesses like Whirlpool Corp, and their investors reason to be alert. Various proxy fight's also occurred which are defined as a technique used by an acquiring company. This occasionally appropriates an attempt to gain control of a takeover "target company", but these conflicts of proxy statements, and or even a possible vote most times are too late when proper evaluations are not considered. These are misguided issues from the bad decisions that the board of directors or high level executives can make which can cause harmful problems. Considering some businesses that fought to survive, this is when the acquiring company or a prosperous business tries to persuade the shareholders. During the 2008 economic crisis various banks consisted of these "target companies" or the business "firms" as takeover concerns with issues. Therefore they then were pondered with circumstantial decisions that management had to make about when a top level individual should be ousted, or the sale of the company had become inevitable.

The format of corporate business is usually in favor of a slate within board of directors favorable to the acquiring company. Understanding this they can control the company without paying a premium price for the firm, and contrary to a few U.S. domestic values some international issues of investments have lately on occasions been proven harmful. This becomes an issue that is not always helpful if the purchasing company is not observant of their merger/buyout goal. The most conflicting and somewhat lawful duty that the SEC, and even the Federal Reserve Bank had (c/o regulators) was when individual U.S. investors filed complaints that were not taken serious. These most times were business minded people expanding their investment resources to advance their disciplines of business value. Therefore this would have more than likely saved more American peoples invested assets of money. Upon this consideration of facts throughout the years small businesses were victimized, and this cost them, and others such as government additional money in the billions of dollars including tax revenue.

A conditional amount of corporate assets in America can be observed within public utility companies, and or the laws within conditions that keep them astute. The public utility industries in America that rarely have any merger or buyout activity consist of services within gas, electricity, communications, water, and (c/o municipalities) wastewater. Observing these services with the utility companies equipment, their assets are managed most always on American soil, and operate under the Public Utility Holding Company Act.

Understanding the rare to nonexistence of utility company merger/buyouts the Public Utility Holding Company Act has given the public utility companies divesture that keeps regulated businesses from operating in an unregulated format of sectored business operating concerns. The Public Utility Holding Company Act (1935) and other "Holding Company" laws were major issues of U.S. legislature which in some capacity appropriated the regulating of the securities and exchange industry. Observing this it reorganized the financial structures of "Holding Companies" in the gas, and electric utilities industry, the banking industry, and the air transportation, and railroad industries which have regulated their debt, and dividend policies. This is the format of how other industries have similar Holding Company" legislative matters. These are the disciplines within the Bank Holding Company Act (1935), the Railroad Holding Companies Act, and the Air Transport Holding Companies Act which all have disciplines that apply to various SEC rules. Then more so the securities and exchange industry of factors within "Holding Company" business values are evaluated with their market and business structure to achieve prosperity. This was observed during the 1930s when abuse by holding companies were rampant, which included diluted stock, top-heavy capital structures with excessive fixed-debt burdens, and manipulation throughout the securities and exchange markets.

Most all holding companies, and U.S. government contractors are publicly traded companies with levels of discipline. This leads to the issues of similarity that a vast amount of engineering firms are privately owned, and have less risk of a business failure. Upon conflicting values they are also not often a target to be bought out with unlawful, and or unreliable control. These companies in the likes of Bechtel Corporation of San Francisco, CA., Sargent & Lundy of Chicago, IL., and a few others being productive American Architecture, and Engineering firms hold high disciplines of engineering for government, and utility companies. These are firms that have built railroads, dams, utility plants, and nuclear power plants. All nuclear plants were authorized by the Atomic Energy Act of 1946 creating vital American assets throughout the electrical power distribution industry. Considering this technology in America the Act also established the United States Atomic Energy Commission to regulate nuclear energy apart from the international ban on nuclear weapons. The United Nations played an important role by establishing the International Atomic Energy Agency (IAEA) which was created in 1956. This international agency was established in order to encourage the peaceful development of nuclear energy with various technology disciplines, while also providing international safeguards against nuclear proliferation. These became the resources that America (c/o international allies) have established within asset developments such as nuclear energy.

Various American made dams, and railroads have been vital assets over the decades from 1900 to 2000 which play vital parts in American industry, and it's U.S. infrastructure. Some strong companies and or firms within these developments have been General Electric Corp, U.S. Steel Corp, Bechtel Corporation, and a few others going between various U.S. sectors of "private and public" owned companies. Also this includes thousands of small, mid-sized, and large architectural, engineering, and construction businesses. Conditionally these are important professional businesses as long as they do good work, and invest in their business in cost effective ways. On occasions these businesses find themselves being part of a merger to improve the level of business that they conduct within operating disciplines. After the 2007 mortgage crisis a certain amount of these companies had to restructure to survive, just like some larger businesses, corporations, and or local governments.

Observing the concept of these small expanding or productive American businesses, most all have consisted of a logical amount of protection which starts with these business owners, and the responsibilities of government. This becomes a factor similar to the U.S. Constitution observing that most all of these conditions of government and business working together with all details must be just right without destructive concern or manipulative conflicts. These disciplines became part of the laws which are the responsibility of the U.S. Department of Justice, the Judiciary, and other state and federal government officials providing manageable resources to govern. Throughout the United States and some other well developed countries, the highest format of technology, and obtaining information illegally has sometimes been traumatic. This means that government has to redress its own commitment to protecting the privacy rights issue of the American society, and the general public.

One example of obtaining information illegally is how Raytheon Corporation was accused by a corporate firm called AGES Group to manipulate biding contract procedures. This was the format of a firm that bid against Raytheon Corp for a $450 million dollar contract with the U.S. Department of Defense which ended up in the U.S. Federal Court in Alabama. AGES alleged that Wackenhut Corp, hired by Raytheon used video, and audio surveillance to spy on the consulting firm hired by AGES to help it prepare for its bid. AGES also said that stolen confidential pricing documents were turned over to Raytheon to manipulate the contract bidding process in Raytheon's favor. The Federal Court of Alabama ruled in favor of AGES, and the larger company within Raytheon had to settle the (felony) case by paying $3 million dollars to the AGES Group, and purchase $13 million dollar's-worth of AGES aircraft parts to settle the case. This illegal scientific factor against the human concept of ambition, and the U.S. Constitution seems lately to have served 5 good issues, and then on occasions the repercussion has victimized

10 to 20 other businesses, and American social concerns. These are people of the American general public whom may be in the process of vital business matters, and or logical social disciplines that have suffered conflicting, and disastrous investment or business results.

As this concept of illegal activity exist like with Raytheon, and even sometimes similar to mergers, and or corporate buyouts that occur, various issues of obtaining information illegally, manipulation, and also fraud have also consisted of insider trading issues. These levels of manipulation, and conflict in a secured information environment have taken billions of dollars of corporate, and more so personal assets in various directions. Another form of corporate manipulation occurs occasionally within the various names, and trademarks of a corporation, organization, collage, or university, and other groups. This even includes government which becomes hopeful not to mislead the American general public. These are legal rights protected under the 1st Amendment of the U.S. Constitution. The format within duties of the Trademark Office in Washington D.C. applies registration of a Trademark on the Principal Registration in the Patent and Trademark Office which provides claim of ownership to everyone's acknowledgement.

Some American trademarks may be observed within companies like Hewlett-Packard with the (hp), General Electric with the (GE), Playboy with the (Bonny, Ears, and Playmate) similar to Ms. USA, and American Telephone & Telegraph with "AT&T and or the other trademark at&t". Contrary to the NBA, NFL, PGA, or LPGA, and or those within professional or semi-professional Baseball, these Symbols or Letters have a Legal Right of authentication. Even the Radio Corporation of America Inc (c/o RCA & the DOG with a Music Box) held vital legal, and social values. A few of the strongest Trademark names seems to be GE, AT&T, Playboy, Kodak, Newsweek, Girl Scouts, Boy Scouts, and a variation of others. These are the factors of a trademark that consist of the exclusive rights that are attached to a registered mark or alphabets within business representation. Observing these registered "trademarks, symbols, or abbreviated letters" within identification, this identified item or symbol can be enforced by lawful action for trademark infringement laws. Some tort law infringements within common law values are considered for unregistered trademarks (c/o corporate associations) upon which most all are representing a strong discipline of lawful, or professional support to be recognized.

For a number of years Norelco (owned by Philips Co.) was a company name brand whom makes electric shavers, and other cosmetic products that went through issues within a business name conflict. This occurred throughout various legal protection matters during the 1940s. The business naming conflict consisted of Philco Company (the Philadelphia Storage Battery Co) whom went through various name changes later in the years was legally able to prevent Philips Co (a European business) from using the name "Philips" on various products in America. Throughout these conditions of the Philco Company whom was also a competitor, they held the legal rights to the name Philips as it applies to trademark rights on their consumer electronic products to be marketed, and sold in the United States. The infringement was applied because the two names were judged, and considered to sound similar.

Observing the Philips Companies decisions to overcome this infringement clause, it resulted in Philips Company using the name Norelco which is the acronym for "North American Philips {electrical} Company". Throughout the decades following, in the late 1940s Philips continued to use the name Norelco for all of their other U.S. distributed products until 1974 when Philips Company purchased the U.S. business Magnovox Company. Soon after this the Philips Co. relabeled their U.S. consumer products to the Magnovox name, but retrained the Norelco name for their other U.S. consumer products. This was under the Magnovox name, but they retrained the Norelco name for their other U.S. marketed products.

During 1981 Philips Company bought out the Philco Company which gave them control of all the trademarks, and the overall assets, and operating capacity of the company. After this purchase the name Norelco was phased out as the parent company name title then they were able to use the Philips Company in America as a name for all of their U.S. products. Considering customer loyalty, and some product patient concerns they chose to retain the Norelco name brand for personal care appliances, and the Magnovox name for economy-priced consumer electronics.

Philips being established during 1891 by Dutch Industrialist Gerard Philips, and Magnovox being founded in 1917 by Edwin Pridham, and Peter Jensen these two companies have long histories that even include assets within defense products. Considering Philips Co. had become a worldwide company from Europe, and Magnovox Co. whom was operated, and established in the United States with some products sold in other countries, various Magnovox assets where established for the U.S. Department of Defense whom remained independent. This independent discipline of the business was named the Magnovox Electronic Systems for defense. Therefore within these two companies that operated in America, and one European company with asset values that applies to technology, they have been somewhat a shared factor of business discipline. This was established between the United States government, and the government in various parts of Europe.

The concept of Magnovox Electronic Systems which stayed independent between issues of defense, and the Philips Co. with their ownership later became part of the Carlyle Group until it was acquired by Hughes Electronic in 1995. Magnovox Electronic Systems consisted of technology within "command, control, and communications with Electronic Warfare, and Sonobuoys equipment. Observing the Hughes Electronics Company that sold their aerospace, and defense operations to Raytheon, this included the Magnovox defense operations that where transferred within ownership as well. Not too long after this, the Raytheon Corporation spun off Sonobuyo operation to create Under Sea Systems. This business which was later known as Ultra-SSI operated in Columbia City, Indiana. The remainder within this business operation is now part of the many operations managed by Raytheon Corporation within their Network Centric Systems in Fort Wayne, Indiana.

CHAPTER SIX
FOREIGN RELATION'S AND JUNK
BOND ISSUES OF VALUE

||||||||||||||||||||||||||||||||||||||||||||||||||||||||||||

Observing the American system of government it has always been important to recognize good, and bad foreign relations that conditionally apply to American businesses. During the last three decades up until 2011 various foreign corporations have been seeking control of American corporate businesses with corporate mergers, and more so buyouts. These issues have vital conditions of awareness, and or have been recognized with the discipline of various laws for professionals, the U.S. Constitution, and even national security which is protecting the American society, and its people. With the increase of Gross National Product in other countries such as China, Japan, Korea, and a few other countries these become vital concerns of how the American economy will be productive for the majority of American citizens. These foreign countries, and businesses are accumulating large values of foreign, and domestic liquidity. Considering them earning American money (c/o the currency rate) their values of liquidity are even being used to buy American companies, and small businesses especially when they are rated as Junk Bond values. This becomes the factor with logical business where various American business owners must continue to expand their resources of business managing disciplines to secure U.S. Constitutional values.

Foreign relations in America has been a critical conflict which applies to business in the U.S. since the years of the Great Depression with a vast amount of American corporate businesses that had to restructure. The United States government has had to make legislative progress which consisted of issues such as unions, Social Security, Workman Compensation, and laws for better market disciplines. Within this factual condition and process the U.S. Securities and Exchange Commission was also established with the Federal Reserve Bank system to create more stability in the U.S. economy. These factors during the Woodrow Wilson Presidential administration began given the American currency leverage, and this provided a logical format for the banking industry to conditionally become more responsible. The Junk Bond market issues within rating of companies becomes valuable when their assets are considered workable by another company similar to LG Electronics Inc. who found this concern in the assets, and products at the Zenith Corporation. Zenith Corporation consisted of revenue earnings slightly above $430 million dollars during 1999, and a bulk of those earnings could have come from U.S. government contracts.

Contrary to LG Electronics completion of the buyout purchase of the Zenith Corporation during 1999 the company LG Electronics established themselves as a multi-billion dollar Korean company, "operating worldwide". This has become a trend with other foreign businesses such as Nippon Steel, Sony, Toyota, and a few others controlling worldwide market values as well. LG Electronics also has been around at least since 1956, which means they have extensive experience in manufacturing, and sales of a variation of electronic products.

A competitive observation can be recognized when their LG Electronic product brands expanded throughout the United States during the 1960s, and 1970s. Before this, the Gold Star Company, and a brand name was changed throughout the procedures of mergers by two Korean companies "Lucky Co., and Gold Star Co." to become LG Electronics. This became the observation of when

LG Electronics started acquiring Zenith Corporation's outstanding shares of stock. Observing this factor the Zenith Corporation was becoming a weaker business which consisted of them having problems staying out of bankruptcy, and this gave them a rating value as a junk bond issue.

As the United States fought in the Korean War during 1951 to 1953 as an ally to help, and defend South Korea against North Korea this was a long-term commitment from a communist country with issues that still consist of various threats. One of North Korea's major threats was the possible proliferation of nuclear technology that includes nuclear guided missile testing which conditionally violates the International Atomic Energy Agency (IAEA) laws. These are the 2010 United Nations (UN) international laws of proliferated war, and or defense activities that North Korean's Supreme Leader Kim Jung II, and others must comply with as a U.N. constituent of good standings. Then even though Kim Jung II has been part of the ruling party since 1948 there has been some understanding of these international laws that must be complied with. Considering North Korea has been accused of working on certain nuclear guided missiles, this illegal process against international laws was established by the IAEA which gives the United Nations authority to even conduct international court proceedings. Therefore this has put the IAEA, and the United Nations in a position to consider sanctions against North Korea.

The United States government has a legal discipline that most times consists of an evaluation not to allow American corporate businesses with technology to help foreign countries to develop nuclear weapons. Even more so they send experts from the U.S. Nuclear Regulatory Commission (NRC), and certain U.N. government officials from the IAEA into these communist, and or other types of governed countries to investigate their lawful or unlawful nuclear (Atomic) developments. These are industry factors from communist countries, and even as they do business in United States, the communist way of life becomes a conflicting issue. This format of international law was established not to destroy the lawful disciplines of the U.S. Constitution, and or its domestic tranquility (c/o international laws) with prosperity.

The conflicting part of a business in various communist countries usually includes government ownership of most of these foreign corporations. This becomes the understanding that various communist countries consist of economic values upon which the states (c/o government) owns most all logical assets. The assets that they own are the land, banks, natural resources, and industry including large-scale trade, and even transportation resource assets that have income generating values, or social concerns. These communist country issues of ownership are now in a resourceful capacity of conflict which includes the fact that government owns most levels of production of certain items, and revenue which funds government, and business. This also includes strict guidelines within the U.S. Media's free speech, and their access to the internet. Cuba, China, North Korea, Vietnam, and Russia are communist countries with economic values upon which the United States government from time to time reserves caution about within their indifferent activities.

The oil industry in America has a vast amount of U.S. petroleum corporations with drilling, production, and exploration of oil and gas from overseas in places like Libya, and upon which these U.S. businesses are usually ready to leave an unsafe region due to war like issues. Libya's army, and their traitorous, and former leader Muammar Gaddafi during 2011 has staged an attack of killing his own citizens. These were citizens that protested against the issues they don't agree with, and his observed lack of capability, and style of leadership in their government. He was killed months later by Libyan rebels. The U.S. President Barack Obama and his administration observed this problem with national defense support, and concern. This included Secretary of State Hillary Clinton, U.N. Ambassador Susan Rice, and others in the United Nations whom have agreed, and ordered air strikes against Gaddafi, and this has caused casualties to his terrorizing army. These factors became relevant for U.S. companies in that region like ConocoPhillips Corporation, ExxonMobil Corporation, and other American contractors conducting business in Libya to be cautious about maintaining their business activity in this region. These are deadly peacekeeping missions pursed by the U.N. and U.S. allied forces for the contractors in the region that are being threatened while the people as citizens are being killed or severely injured by Muammar Gaddafi's terrorizing troops.

Observing ExxonMobil Corp (c/o the 1999 merger), and the ConocoPhillips Corp (c/o the 2002 merger) these 4 companies that became 2 larger businesses was the result from their future concern of economic values. My opinion is that certain accidents have also cost them severely within liability expenses, and legal fees. The Exxon Valdez oil spill in the Alaskan Bay (c/o 1989) cost Exxon Corporation hundreds of millions of dollars. Both Exxon and Mobil Oil Corporation where established from the Standard Oil Corporation with John D. Rockefeller more so being a decedent to the establishment of Exxon Oil Corporation. This was due to the massive size of Standard Oil being broken down over the years which means sense 1911 they have experienced various issues of change in the U.S. oil industry. Also some people have been known to say these mergers where pursed to become the largest oil company's in world. This formal condition in America has also included certain conflicts in the steel industry which is starting to become a trend with good and bad results.

One opinion about becoming the largest worldwide or American corporation appropriating various products and or service resources in certain individual market sectors like oil or steel production, this has also been considered to offset foreign competition. Observing this has become the issue of were some OPEC members have been a challenge, and conflict to U.S. Anti-Trust laws of the United States. This also includes how they have tried to take control of numerous businesses other than those in the oil industry throughout America. These transactions with conflicting concerns that emerged from issues in America, and conflicting support for places such as Libya, India, and Iraq have also been part of Americas increased problem of international investments that have also included international terror.

Lakshmi Mittal of Arcelor-Mittal Steel Group (c/o ISG) has bought out all active steel mill companies in the Midwest of the United States except for U.S. Steel Corporation, and some privately owned smaller steel factories. Over the last 30 years up to 2005 the loss of American steel manufactures within Bethlehem Steel, and Inland Steel were purchased by Mittal. Prior to this LTV, and J&L whom were part of conflicting losses, they also became part of this purchase agreement which was a consolidation of steel mill assets. These losses included vital complications that were also purchase agreements (c/o ISG) by Mittal. During the 1950s, and 1960s all 4 of these companies did well as productive American corporate businesses. This is part of a conflicting loss within U.S. defense contractors with specialty metals from U.S. defense contract concerns. These also are vital issues upon which these steel companies are now occasionally relocating their headquarters overseas. This conditionally includes some small businesses expanding into resourceful corporations that were held back from expansion disciplines, and resources of economic development. Observing Lakshmi Mittal and him being from India (c/o the Middle East) this has raised questions about how committed he is to the U.S. Constitution, the U.S. citizens, and the American system of government conditionally making America suffer a severe loss.

Understanding these factors between the American steel industry, and more so certain U.S. oil companies, and the Organization of Petroleum Exporting Countries (OPEC) that occasionally operate in America has done so with conflict. Some of these conflicts go back as far as the oil embargo of 1973 up until recently with the control of large and small businesses that have compounded vital issues in the American society of business. Another factor is how during 1990 to 1998 thousands of American gas stations were purchased by people from the Middle East eliminating a high percentage of ownership from American owners, and converting this market into somewhat an illegal "cultural business monopoly". Besides gas stations and other businesses these conflicts included them not having to pay taxes for seven years. Then in America it came be recognized that this tax revenue issue, foreign conflicts, and the terrorist attacks within September 11, 2001 was part of a loss exceeding well over a trillion dollars easily with these conflicts.

Contrary to this tremendous value within losses on September 11, 2001 the U.S. government also was losing tax revenue. Other losses included people, and assets between business and government upon which 10 years later the Pentagon still needs repairs from the 9-11 Report of damage. This was also observed especially from local small businesses in America which included these new business owners that became active in sending money to terrorist infected countries. This capacity of money being sent back to their home land throughout conflicting regions in the Middle East is a National Security threat due to the fact that this is where America has been fighting a war from 2002 thru 2011. Within the relevant concern of these issues, certain American regions have accumulated an increase of more Middle Eastern born business owners than American citizen proprietors in a vast amount of U.S. regions. Therefore this equation is unbalanced with people losing in business whom were born into various American small businesses, and this includes a loss of other industry opportunities.

The issue of OPEC, and certain people that worked for the United Nations in New York City, and even those working with responsibilities for the U.S. Federal Trade Commission between Chicago, Washington D.C. and a few other regions had seem to ignore U.S. Anti-Trust laws. Even though this becomes a duty of the U.S. Department of Justice's (DOJ) Anti-Trust division, these and other government entities could have been more observant about these laws that were established in the 1920s. This was a tremendous conflict in business that was not recognized by Anna Bingaman head of the DOJ's Anti-Trust divisions in the 1990s. This slowly became a problem before some of these conflicts pushed various important American small business owner's full speed backwards.

William Daly is one of a vast amount of people within business, and as government officials that indirectly supported certain foreign enemy agendas that took these conflicts to a record capacity of disaster. This can even be observed with the City of Chicago losing corporate offices, and various business operations including its headquarters of

Amoco Oil Corporation. He did this by instigating various conflicts of interest (with satellite communication systems unlawfully) that manipulated a vast amount of American small businesses. These businesses were victimized, and this made them vulnerable against American business owner disciplines that supported enemy agendas, and foreign ownership of American businesses. This also seems to be the reason (c/o an Endless Loop Crisis) that Ameritech Corp with William Daly did not survive as a communication's company for more than 10 years.

At the present time OPEC, and its 12 member countries, and their citizen issues within business owners have cause suffering, and have instigated conflicts in the United States with destructive support from certain Americans. This discrepancy occurred from certain levels of hate, and animosity between some American's causing deceptive problems which has increased with foreign, and or domestic illegal and hazardous use of commercial satellites, and terrorist like acts. This format of bad technology was (c/o financial and violent acts of crime) instigated by conflicts of interest from William Daly, Karen F. Wilson and others with similar technology as Ameritech Corporation. These issues were some of the worse business, and government decisions in American history. Apart from conflicting technology these American issues with problems between Saudi Arabia, and more so Libya including Iraq providing oil and gas to the United States, and other countries has consisted of occasional harm. The factual harm is through American Constitutional values of economic liquidity with U.S. Anti-Trust law violations. These issues of liquidity, and certain U.S. Constitutional law disciplines were seriously ignored during the tenures of Anna Bingaman at the Anti-Trust division with Attorney General Janet Reno. This concern has provided American currency to people like Saddam Hussein, and other terrorist in that region of the world which included Osama Bin Laden.

The concept of these foreign relation conflicts have provided harm to American Constitutional values of economic liquidity, and prosperity. This has become a problem that affected the steel, oil, air travel, and the communications industry of America which has suffered setbacks with a vast amount of business owners within their effort to establish any kind of business progress. Observing these factors certain American oil companies have observed terrorism closer than the United States government until the observed terrorist attack of September 11, 2001. Therefore the effect on "American soil" being a crime against the United States was tremendously unusual upon which has caused destructive harm to American citizens, businesses, and government.

Before, and more so following these 9-11 Report terrorist attacks various American corporate businesses found themselves more and more in financial trouble. This was evident in the U.S. business sectors of the airline industry, the automobile industry, and even the banking industry with vast amounts of employed people being laid off, and losing vital assets. The following six months after these 9-11 Report attacks GM, Ford, and Chrysler Corporation consisted of automobile sales which became tremendously slow. This was a problem almost up until the following years of 2010 which still caused an excess of automobile inventory. Chrysler Corporation was then hit the worse throughout the American automobile industry sense the September 11, 2001 attacks which led to their merger/buyout conditional agreement from Fiat years following whom is an Italian auto maker.

Considering the American airline industry the U.S. government has increased spending at well over a few billion dollars for airport security. These factors become relevant with the newly established U.S. Department of Homeland Security as well certain activities at the U.S. Department of Transportation which included "TSA" which is the Transportation Security Administration. This factor becomes a relevant observation within the concern that the Chrysler Corporation, and more so United Airlines Inc., and American Airlines Inc. still holds disciplines as American corporate businesses that were victimized. The factual observation of these economic troubles for business is observed while the other auto companies, and the airline industry including connected companies have struggled to restructure in a different capacity then they did decades before.

One of the few industries contrary to terrorism that did not suffer badly was the American pharmaceutical industry within companies like Pfizer Inc., Eli Lilly & Company, and a few others. The Pfizer Inc. Company did so well that in 2009 they bought out one of their most competitive rivals, the Wyeth Company for an agreed cost of $68 billion dollars, and invested additional billions in other "research and development" projects. Some executives at Pfizer Inc. besides their former CEO Jeff Kinder said that actually (Pfizer) the company may have a problem within becoming too big for logical management. Then Eli Lilly & Company's business activity with the purchase of Imclone Inc. was just as expensive with Eli Lilly & Company paying $6.5 billion for the Imclone pharmaceutical company. Observing this, very few if any foreign businesses have yet to buyout, or have taken any majority control of any American pharmaceutical company. Even during the 2008 economic crisis most U.S. pharmaceutical corporate businesses have done well. Therefore the pharmaceutical industry in America has held steady with overall growth.

The vast amount of research and development that a certain amount of American companies pursues is part of their increasing wealth with Patent Rights of products protected through the U.S. Government's Patent office. Considering this also happens in well-developed foreign countries applicable to various businesses the United States has still maintained various levels of achievements that are beneficial to society. Most of these product achievements are then copied or matched in other countries that apply to conflicting values of business. Apple Inc. is a valuable example with their iphone, the ipod, and other products such as computers. Some of their products along with other companies have been recognized as being developed in the black markets of phony products from places such as China, and other countries. They even then manufacture these illegal products apart from some legitimate foreign companies that may establish their own products within technology.

Understanding global business issues that have an effect on the American society, various businesses, and other well developed countries are structured by a matter of laws, work ethics, and logical disciplines of business. These business factors are found in the clothing industry, the automobile industry, the food industry, and even subjects like candy, farm produce, alcohol, tobacco, and firearms. Even as these issues of product supply, and demand become a retail store issue of high volume sales, then market values may even be matched for sales on the internet. This becomes the concept of manufacturing and corporate business concerns with some companies becoming junk bond issues if management does not regroup and this occasionally will play a role within a pass or fail rating. Therefore the strongest and most lawful companies will continue to help other businesses survive when needing a change in management or a full restructuring is important apart from being rated as a junk bond issue.

CHAPTER SEVEN
A TRANSITION OF AMERICAN
DEFENSE CONTRACTORS

IIIIIIIIIIIIIIIIIIIIIIIIIIIIIIIIIIIIIIIIIIIIIIIIIIIIIIIIIIIII

The United States Department of Defense, the Department of Homeland Security, and the overall U.S. federal government that applies to the American society of people depend on our American resources of corporate businesses whom are active defense contractors. These become vital issues to provide various levels of U.S. national security issues of employment, and defense product resources throughout the United States. A vast amount of U.S. defense contractors that are reviewed by the U.S. Defense Secretary go back more than 100 years. Most all of these businesses whom are government contractors that have survived consisted of technology values that have changed with the times, and this includes their economic decisions that are vital to be a workable level of progress.

Another resource within the changing times includes the United States history of war and defense which goes back to the 1700s. These conditional government changes have went from the first establishment of the United States War Department who recognized, and appointed the U.S. Secretary of War as being Henry Knox in 1789. Then the United States government in 1947 established the U.S. Department of Defense along with the title Secretary of Defense. The first Secretary of Defense was James Forrestal whom was from New York, and now during 2012 Leon Panetta has been appointed as Defense Secretary.

The newly established U.S. Department of Homeland Security has some similar concerns even with the appointment of Homeland Security advisors. Over the last 10 years from 2001 the Homeland Security Department has consisted of 5 appointed advisors. These advisors have started with Tom Ridge being the first, and today's present (2012) advisor being John Brennan. Understanding, and evaluating new security measures they operate with their own budget that is approved annually by the U.S. Congress. Observing these departments today within the U.S. federal government whom spends billions of dollars a year on various defense business contractors throughout America, this therefore becomes a vital part of the American economy with some argumentative concerns.

A certain amount of these companies have been shuffled around as their parent companies have went out of business, or they were bought out by a company that the United States considers not qualified to be a U.S. Defense Department contractor. These factual defense resource's also includes a few select foreign contractors that the U.S. Department of Defense may buy products from, but American companies are held with the highest levels of valued security, and contract product consideration. Then therefore the condition of government disciplines for national security are somewhat protected.

The logical resource within qualifications of U.S. defense contractors is similar to companies like Boeing, General Dynamics, Raytheon, General Electric, AM General, and a conditional amount of others. These conditions that are observed also consist of the amount of the time that these contractors are part of the buy, and sale process within mergers and acquisitions. Observing these strong productive companies, other corporate businesses with losses including some of their diversified product divisions are most times sold to other traditional American companies that are, or can be qualified as U.S. defense contractors. Therefore all businesses involved including any new foreign parent company of conflict "with", or more so "without" the defense business, or division can be rewarded most logical benefits that these companies share financially. Then upon the buy or sale acquisition of a defense business which must include American professionals, citizens, or certain people, these are the lawful considerations of an affiliated constituent to the United State government. This level of transitional business is then valued within these factors of American companies which becomes the better level of observation that most U.S. national security values can be protected with better expansion.

As the years, and decades have went on up to the millennium of 2000 various U.S. defense military contractors have created advanced products within various disciplines of engineering, and technology. These factors of advancement have provided billions and trillions of dollars into the American economy. During 2010 the United States Military expenditures cost was over $698 billion dollars upon which U.S. Defense Security Robert Gates has reportedly said; this military spending needs to be adjusted to the changing nature of threats from enemy nations. This was apparent during the tenure of Donald Rumsfeld whom was the Secretary of Defense on September 11, 2001 when airplanes were hijacked, and crashed into the Pentagon, the World Trade Centers, and with one airplane from Ohio crashing into a field in Pennsylvania. This attack was different, but similar from various Middle Eastern hijackings of commercial airplanes in the 1970s, and 1980s which also became part of the 2001 attacks which outlined the beginning of the American war in Iraq, and Afghanistan.

Sense the early 1990s (contrary to 2001) a vast amount of corporations are finding themselves in bankruptcy, or they are valued as a junk bond issue that must be restructured. These corporate businesses apply to the U.S. financial markets which consist of the consideration of will they survive in business which becomes a direct concern for the U.S. government, and not to mention their American employees. The United States Department of Defense takes observation of these factors, and then starts to evaluate the company's defense business to have a proxy board for national security reasons. This is vital when a foreign person or business seeks opportunities to buy an American company that manages a certain amount of classified information. These issues upon appropriate decisions are information details that most "National Governments" work to manage, and in the United States this is observed as a legal discipline that was established by Executive Orders of the U.S. Presidency.

Observing the mid-west of the United States which has various companies with a critical pass in U.S. defense contracts, certain levels of overall concern about business ownership must be reviewed. This factor within corporate businesses consist of how changes occurred at LTV Corporation, Inland Steel Corp, Zenith Corp, Chrysler Corp and a few others. Even the prevailing factors of a company from England (c/o the British) being a close ally to the U.S. government is not the most secured decision or activity of protecting American businesses, and society from losses. The Amoco Oil Corporation buyout from British Petroleum (c/o BP America), and its corporate business transaction included their U.S. defense contract work to be reconsidered. Therefore even though the contract was still honored, this transaction pushed a vast amount of American business values backwards.

The concentration of a vast amount of American employees, and executives like in the U.S. oil industry with a scaled down corporate raider, and business professional like T-Boone Pickens (c/o American business proxies) was part of changes that transitioned certain business values. He became the founder of BP Capital, and this carried relevant defense product, and contract qualifications with the U.S. government, and a blessing from the British government. Upon this observation which kept the U.S. government at ease, a certain amount of other American employees involved established a quota. Then Bob Dudley their CEO at BP whom was born as an American citizen included another vast amount of U.S. government values of support for defense and government contract work. Some of these values were observed to be a logical consideration, and reason why he was chosen as the predecessor of Tony Haywood whom is British, but their new business activity in the U.S. was struggling with accidents, and liability issues in the courts. The struggle more so consisted of vital disciplines to improve their business activity within work place liabilities that conditionally consisted of fatal accidents that cost them a tremendous amount of money.

This was the time when Bob Dudley with various BP board members, and officials of President Barack Obama's administration began working close together with argumentative factors after BP's 2nd bad accident during 2010. Considering this issue of CEO reorganizing after the BP 2010 Gulf of Mexico fatal "explosion, and severe oil leek disaster", this was factored as a vital problem of liquidity that needed to change. As this applies to defense contracts they have left Exxon Corporation (c/o ExxonMobil) as one of the major oil, and gas U.S. defense contractors. Considering this acquisition by BP whom is the largest oil company in England, the elimination of Amoco Oil Corporation became a tremendous corporate buyout issue for various American employees, and contractors whom still seem to be making adjustments of equity, and liability. Contrary to their core product business activity, their defense contract requirement disciplines changed especially when it applies to national security, and defense contract values throughout Loudon, England, apart from the U.S. government.

Observing various defense contractors in the states of Indiana, Illinois, Ohio, and Michigan certain people and technology has consisted of values that have changed these regions economically. Considering various mid-size companies that have went bankrupt, or who were purchased by foreign businesspeople a vast amount of economic development also went back to some of their home countries. A loss of American business owners consist of factors which included the economy in cities like Gary, Indiana; Detroit, Michigan; Cleveland, Ohio; Harrisburg, Pennsylvania, and a few others. This was observed at the extent that war time manufacturing production losses have closed 1000s of factories sense the 1970s. These businesses with factories, and a few other issues such as new manufacturing technology that use fewer employees have transformed cities into a tremendous conflict of ghostly existence.

Actually as we observe more businesses with productive management, it is important that we could have provided a more diversified level of civilian, and defense products that could have provided a better economic overall effect. These complications with small and large businesses also became a vital issue concerning government tax revenue, but innovation issues and the courts did not keep up with this vital process. Then the importance of "defense items" that were produced at different rates due to the fact that certain defense manufacturing divisions or core product business operations may be moved to the east, west, or to southern parts of the United States from the mid-west became a logical conflict to the region's economy. Considering these factors the worse conditions that included outsourcing jobs to foreign countries had to be reevaluated. Therefore if a foreign business person or company took control of an American business, all workable ideas in America including technology would lose a level of secured format within social, and business disciplines. This becomes logical to manufacturing, and national security corrections which had to be made by businesses, and the U.S. government.

The most logical way some of these transactions occurred is when a corporation will only take over the plant, and location of where most of the defense product manufacturing operations are conducted. Observing this the economic development has been shifted into a foreign concept of ideas that sometimes are not within the best interest of the United States. This even includes phony or illegal defense products or even mechanical parts made outside of the United States for important U.S. made boats, and aircrafts that become dangerous in some factual terms of liability. Contrary to liability issues of mechanical parts from various foreign countries, they usually are established with high levels of quality. This is then a factor of satisfaction to the U.S. government, and the general public of people as consumers apart from products made for the U.S. Department of Defense. Within this process, the timing factor on occasions is a value within other lawful products with conditional progress which is important when doing business with the U.S. federal government, and other internationally governed concerns, or allies.

Contrary to American corporations creating these defense products faster than we did years ago, safety, and liability including their core origination of corporate products has still been an important issue within business factors. This also becomes a logical factor of why American standards, and specifications in most U.S. business product designs, and manufacturing are appropriately set, and considered as qualified for American defense required product use activity. Considering the economic changing times within regional, and national economics that has offered additional concerns, and challenges these become valued adjustments from research and product development. Then this also improves the way of normal, and valued conditions of life existence in the American society which is part of domestic tranquility for conditions of public safety or protection. These workable commitments that Americans find, and seek consist of values within all conditions of a corporations overall business plan, and levels of process developments. Then this also becomes the important process of lawfully safe businesses that have established a format, and discipline to survive. Therefore various reasons (c/o internal and external safety) can cause the publicly held company to become targeted by an issue of a corporate merger or hostile takeover. This then would include appropriate or negotiated agreements with value from a corporate raider, or other interested corporate businesses.

Understanding higher liability standards are achieved with productive work; various companies provide a dependent level of resources on the stability, and or their expansion opportunities. These values of resourceful work disciplines become dependable as they make decisions or as they may feel various changes are important to pursue. Observing Zenith Corporation, and Amoco Oil Corporation these where defense contractors, and businesses that manufactured products with high standards. Before the merger/ buyout of these two companies which included their resources of expansion supporting the American economy their issues of management, and labor occasionally had concerns. The most important concern was not to destroy the vital conditions of their business existence, and their process of production.

The most valued condition of business occurred over the decades which have given American defense contractors business activity commitments that are closely monitored by government, and the laws of the U.S. Constitution. Upon these facts the confidence of the American society within products used by civilians, and or the U.S. military are astute, and valued with liability. Some of this technology is developed even through the National Aeronautics and Space Administration (NASA) which has conducted experiments that led to important values of technology, and this still consist of vital long-term commitments. Upon this consideration of the U.S. government it becomes important that we then must evaluate the regulated use of these product concerns, and other conditions of technology.

Chrysler Corporation (c/o Fiat) is still manufacturing a vast amount of quality products, but as we observe these 3 companies which includes the vital likes of Zenith Corporation, and a few others with their core product divisions, they did not hold the best format of values in business. This consisted of their levels of production including sales which had suffered due to their ability to hold issues of stability. The Chrysler Corporation has regained their market share of vehicle sales from the economic crisis between 2002 to 2008, but this was somewhat due to help from the U.S. government, the Fiat investment, and certain improvements in the economy. These concerns where factored within problems that consisted of weakening values throughout management, and labor union decisions. Contrary to these issues that were geared towards economics, and product satisfaction within sales various business matters must still hold quality, and ethical standards within their contract business activities. Amoco Oil Corporation became different with a few fatal accidents that consolidated additional liability cost, and losses even after their buyout transaction.

Observing these businesses that include their civilian, and military levels of production, and sales they also took an economic loss when they failed to "hire and train" the best American employees possible. These hiring and training values consist of cost, and commitment factors which become a problem within businesses not having people that learn various production values. Other vital things that they should have learned with clear understanding are the business routine with safety (c/o Amoco), and how to improve vital parts of the operation, and then stay committed to the company. Even the concept of Americans who leave the company after being a very helpful employee is sometimes much more rewarding to the overall American society. This becomes the understanding that sometimes the company then may consist of the repercussion of what a foreign born person might do if they leave an American business, and not have good intensions. Therefore their defense contract business activity is reconsidered in various ways which may be determined over a span of years. Contrary to conflicts this is the vital concept of productive former employees, and how their future activity within defense contracts are part of an overall business, and government format of restructuring, and valued experience.

Understanding the continued changing times certain U.S. defense contractors have become more detailed with business merger/buyout disciplines. This becomes the factor of how some companies have accumulated mostly defense contract work which gives them expertise in this government industry sector of business. Upon this observation the U.S. government, and various state governments recognize that they are part of corporate businesses that have the ability to manage all of the proper disciplines of various U.S. defense project requirements. This mostly includes diversified businesses with the ability to buyout other military product divisions, and or businesses. Understanding this formal concern, General Dynamics, Boeing, Northrop Grumman, Raytheon, Goodrich, General Electric, Lockheed Martin, and various others have engaged fully in extensive projects for the U.S. Department of Defense. This included buying out, and or taking over corporate defense business divisions, and businesses which they have a level of expertise or professional experience with. This vitally applies to the manufacturing, managing, and sales of these products at a lawful, and productive rate.

These business values within corporate activities are logical throughout the industries of aerospace, and defense businesses with manufacturing. Considering these business production resources, their operating value of corporate establishments have a detailed format within working with the United States Army, Navy, Air

Force, Marines, and or Coast Guard to keep them equipped. General Dynamics (c/o Defense), and Northrop Grumman (c/o Aerospace & Defense) over the years have engaged in corporate buyouts, and merger activity productively with numerous companies. One of the few mergers that were not approved by the U.S. government was the considered agreement between Lockheed Martin, and Northrop Grumman to merge during 1998. Considering this type of business merger or agreement being disapproved by the U.S. government is sometimes an issue of anti-trust, but even the government can be wrong which we recognized 3 years after 1998 with the 9-11 Report crisis.

Upon the many other acquisitions of Northrop Grumman they purchased Newport News Shipbuilding apart from a Docking Company which was a private company. Newport News Shipbuilding has built naval ships since the early 1900s up until 2001. Most of this ship building activity was conducted on nearby shipping docks, and at their Newport News, Virginia headquarters, and docking operation were they built numerous large commercial, and more so military battle ship vessels. General Electric, and Westinghouse became important business contract constituents that has sold shipbuilders vast amounts of equipment (c/o meters & instruments) that you can find on these ship vessels as completed projects. This shipbuilding process also included the manufacturing, and steel fabricated parts from contractors with U.S. Steel, the former Inland Steel, and Bethlehem Steel Corporation as ordered agreements.

During 1996 Northrop Grumman acquired Westinghouse Electric Systems which has manufactured radar equipment, radio communication equipment, torpedoes, and other electronic and defense devices sense the 1940s. Westinghouse Electric Corporation had been around sense 1886, and during 1995 they bought out Columbia Broadcasting Corporation (CBS), and then Westinghouse, and both sets of board of directors agreed to change their name to CBS. Following them adding their change of name amendments to CBS with the overall remaining majority of the business became Viacom to become a restructured major television and radio network broadcasting company. This was a logical concept of big business decisions were various markets were involved affecting numerous regions with changes in this American business industry concern. Northrop Grumman also acquired the 100 year old business TRW (Tropical Storm Warning) Inc. to create two business division sectors. These divisions where established as a Space Technology sector, and a Mission System sector business operation with facilities between California, and Virginia. TRW Incorporated also had an Aeronautical division that was sold to Goodrich Corp which increased the aerospace activity business disciplines that the Goodrich Corporation has been establishing, and restructuring during the 1ˢᵗ decade of 2000.

Lockheed Martin Corporation became a vital resource within United States defense contractors from a commitment of work, and various corporate mergers. Before the 1995 merger of Lockheed Corporation and Martin Marietta Corporation these two corporations engaged in various technical engineering projects for corporations, and more so the U.S. government. Martin Marietta Corporation was a leader in chemicals, electronics, and aerospace. The Martin Marietta Corp years later was commissioned to build the Monorail System at Walt Disney World, and various missiles with electronic systems for the U.S. Department of Defense. Two of their many corporate acquisitions consisted of the purchase of GE Aerospace for $3 billion dollars, and a General Dynamics Corp space systems unit, upon which all occurred during 1993 that increased Martin Marietta's aerospace, and defense industry values.

The Lockheed Corporation was an American aerospace company that was established from certain aircraft manufacturing that goes back to around 1912. Then observing the Great Depression, the company went through two name changes, and then with the bad economic times, they fail into receivership. The Lockheed Corporation during the 1930s was then restructured by Robert Gross, and his brother Courtland Gross upon which at that time the company established the name Lockheed Corporation. During World War II in the 1940s Lockheed Corporation produced 19,278 aircrafts that helped win the American war over Japan after the attacks on Pearl Harbor. Observing World War I & II, the Korean

War, and the Vietnam War this business activity consisted of war time production that was good for the American economy contrary to the sad loss of U.S. solders. Some of these defense business activities consisted of companies like Raytheon manufacturing, and selling Patriot missiles, and its operating systems that were used in the first (1991) Persian Gulf War. Observing this, various companies changed with the times, and innovation to become more helpful in future American wars, and defense conflicts.

The transitioning of the American economy with these issues of defense spending from the U.S. government were valuable until things shifted with foreign people taking control of American businesses, and then occasionally supporting an enemy foreign agenda. The most troubling factor within this problem was observed when new U.S. citizens from the Middle East were sending large amounts of money to terrorist regions after the September 11, 2001 attacks. Another conflicting effect consisted of various Middle Eastern investors in America that exercised the sale of hundreds millions of dollars of stock options after these terrorist attacks.

The American society became complacent before the (September) 9-11 Report attack, and due to these new threats the U.S. Department of Homeland Security, and the Transportation Security Administration (TSA) was established in 2002. The Department of Homeland Security consisted of a new administrative Secretary, a former Governor of Pennsylvania Tom Ridge who operated from their first federal government budget at just over $31 billion dollars. Years following up to the year of 2012, the Department of Homeland Security budget had increased to $56 billion dollars annually. Therefore international, and domestic terrorist plots, or even national disasters could then be handled with greater observation, and enforcement of laws to protect the people, and certain American assets.

Contrary to terrorism U.S. domestic issues within small arms such as handguns, and rifles including ammunition manufacturing have been vital defense business operations. This became the importance of companies like Remington Arms Company Inc., Bushmaster Firearms, and the Smith & Wesson Holding Company.

The U.S. defense business within massive guns being purchased from these companies that go back at least one hundred years has always been a procurement of importance. This is the observation of Remington Inc. which was established in 1816, and Smith & Wesson starting their business production in 1852 which gives them decades of U.S. defense, and civil service (c/o police departments) contract experience. Understanding this level of business for defense, and civilian products of armed protection, the laws within the 2nd Amendment may still need some redress through government, and the people of America.

Even though both Remington, and Smith & Wesson are companies with their headquarters in the United States their many firearm products have been sold in various regions throughout the world. The Remington Inc. business for decades has made responsible progress up until them, and Bushmaster Firearms Co where part of a purchasing stake from Cerberus Management, and the Freedom Group. This was done to save these businesses from lawsuits that consisted of conflicting damages were people had been killed by certain products they manufacture, and sale. As it applies to American laws, and the courts these companies still needed the commitment of their corporate officials, and not just owners from Wall Street investment firms.

Contrary to Cerberus Capital Management and their business activities, the Freedom Group is a "manufacturing holding company" that can support various arm dealings in America. This includes issues within the contingent circumstances of a gun manufacturing company, and their legal concerns that have included them working with the state and federal courts, and additional government concerns. Most of the business transactions within contingent mergers had an undisclosed dollar amount that was applied to their agreements. Observing this factor within Cerberus Capital Management, and their many acquisition merger agreements within companies like Chrysler, and GMAC managing these, and others as defense contractors within Bushmaster Firearms, and Remington Inc. became somewhat of a junk bond issue of conflict. This was valued within their core products as being important (c/o liability) to various U.S. defense, civilian, and some civil service activities.

These valued issues of U.S. government "Defense Procurements" are important along with a vast amount of civilian, and defense products. Other important products that go along with vital procurement programs may come from companies such as Texas Instruments Inc. with their laser guided bombs. Also besides manufacturing calculators, their monolithic calculators which includes other electronics from a format of their "Monolithic Microwave Integrated Circuits", and sensors have made them attractive to a corporate investor like Raytheon Corporation. The Texas Instruments Inc. business within circuits, and even more so semiconductors has provided various technology by-products that were products of government recommended divesture. This level of divesture also includes certain technology between companies such as Raytheon, and other exploratory technology between companies such as Eastman Kodak, Allied Signal and Motorola's institutional methodology. Considering these factors including the methodology of certain values of technology supported by the United States government these issues have developed a logical format of diversified defense products. These various conditions of research and methods can implement the factual levels of new and old combined technology to create better defense, and other resourceful civilian products to aid the American society.

In 2011 Texas Instruments Inc. bought out National Semiconductor which is a company that has advanced for decades manufacturing semiconductors as bi-products for a variation of companies. Observing the company Texas Instruments, and their manufacturing of instrumentation products of circuit, and digital electronic items this capacity of products has been a productive resource of their business sense the 1930s. Their consumer, and U.S. defense business dealings have kept them as a vitally productive corporate business to purchase other businesses and create better electronic products. The buyout purchase of National Semiconductor by Texas Instruments also has given this large company additional strength within markets such as wireless headsets, and electronic displays. Also a variety of parallel sectors within medicine, automobile parts, industries similar to robotics, and test measurement equipment are part of product upgrades that will more than likely occur. Therefore another business has potentially expanded from a corporate buyout.

CHAPTER EIGHT
SMALL BUSINESSES, CORPORATIONS, AND WORKABLE JUNK BONDS

||||||||||||||||||||||||||||||||||||||||||||||||||||||||||||||||||||||||||||||

Throughout the American society we live in (c/o 2001 to 2012) small businesses are taking a severe beating, while some large corporations are buying more businesses, and or corporate divisions that they consider workable. This most times becomes a combination of business adjustments that they can prosper from with simple input, and output factors of progress which includes their resource of employees. Understanding this, the concept of transactions has become more complex lately with conflicting issues, and the format of sometimes needing government requirements, and approval to buy and maintain a controlling stake in certain junk bond business issues. Also this occasionally is a subject that must be settled thru the courts when buyouts or mergers are a perceptional issue. This is the format, and consideration that these businesses are vulnerable during their first few years of business, or during large adjustments to the business operation. Considering these factual adjustments this means they can suffer outside economic conflicts that can be considered a serious crime which must be corrected in an affordable way.

Workable businesses, and potentially good junk bond issues can fail if lawyers, and management officials don't have the most workable disciplines to be helpful to small business issues of stability. This is vital to business issues of expansion that the American society including government requires apart from accepting some exceptional losses that could have been prevented. This level of losses also consist of how small business owners make decisions on investing in other businesses, and even how people grow as small investors that gain value into becoming larger investors. These factors within procedures are similar to small business expansions, but they are investors with a focus to expand their own investments, businesses, or economic resources.

The format of small and large business including junk bond issues within mostly mid-size, and large corporations during the 1st decade of 2000 were sometimes almost begging to be bought out (c/o some bailouts) at the right price. Bankruptcy and receivership are part of the biggest fears that occurred with American International Group, Bear Stearns, Countrywide, Lehman Brothers, and other businesses. This becomes a valued concern when certain business factors are not workable. Some values can be recognized when deregulation helped the 5 largest U.S. banks within Bank of America, Citigroup, JP Morgan, Wachovia, and Wells Fargo increase their assets from $2.2 trillion to $6.8 trillion dollars.

Most aggressive banking activity occurred before the financial crisis applied serve losses to most all of the five largest American banking institutions, and other businesses in 2008. Apart from major investment banks having similar economic growth, and expansion a vast amount of small mortgage lenders in an overbuilt real estate market was part of this conflicting financial growth. Following this, some of the most critical merger/buyout conditions of business acquisitions started to become a savor, which included bargain buyouts recommended by the U.S. government, the FDIC, and a select few others. These seriously bad issues are causing a troubling effect on the American economy which becomes conflicting for the people as workable executives, and productive employees. Considering these facts, and issues of American values of employment with some international conflicts the American society has tried to manage a struggling economy. Then the years to figure out how to recover from the first decade of 2000 have become very complex.

During a different time in American business most mergers and acquisitions were considered in a more prosperous way in which most involved parties within buyers or sellers would benefit. One of the largest corporations that have pursued the buy and sale of smaller corporations, and business divisions to keep accountable books balanced is the General Electric Corporation whom is a conglomerate. During the CEO Jack Welch era at GE Corp a vast amount of their business growth, and restructuring came from corporate buyouts, and a few high profile mergers. These buyouts, acquisitions, and mergers with other corporate businesses such as NBC whom is a strong television network were business transactions that gave GE Corporation additional liquidity, and this provided the government with logical tax revenue. As we observe hardware stores, mini mart gas stations, grocery stores, and major department stores, various GE products with "supply and demand" issues have become helpful to American values, which also provides a "money supply with a money circulation". This money circulation within managing disciplines is vital to Americans, and the existing economy.

Observing other corporate products with a productive money circulation value this becomes part of the American economy with some international, and U.S. domestic retail business values. Also this includes service industry business disciplines with most oil companies, and fast food restaurant chains that have also provided good, and some bad logical small business ownership issues. These businesses as franchises are usually corporate or privately owned, and are rarely considered a junk bond issue. This might include McDonalds, and Burger King Restaurants or Mibas Muffler vehicle repair shops. Other similar businesses are State Farm Insurance, All State Insurance, or H&R Block Tax Services Incorporated. Upon this observation these are businesses that are not always closely associated with the U.S. Small Business Administration which has a logical value to help entrepreneurs, but their small and large business contributions to American commerce is a positive value.

The U.S. Small Business Administration (SBA) was established by the U.S. Congress in 1953 during the Eisenhower presidential administration. Their format of responsibilities consist of values to maintain, and strengthen the viability of small businesses, and by assisting business in the economic recovery of communities after certain natural disasters. These eminent powers of lending, and assistance from the U.S. federal government are vitally useful if all Constitutional values are lawfully applied. Understanding this factor there is a difference between franchises, family businesses and sole proprietors that on occasions when disasters occur all small businesses are granted an evaluation for SBA assistance. These business values sense the 1950s has given some small businesses the support to expand, but the other hard working factor within productive business is the array of decisions by the owners. Most productive American businesses that expand have a disciplined level of ownership to control the amount of logical government activities in their business. The American banking industry during 2008, and 2009 struggled with these concerns through small, and large banks, and even some insurance companies that had very little choice but to have conditional government intervention.

The banking industry, and some insurance companies have been rated as junk bond issues at a higher rate than most other times in the American history of public company ratings. These small and large business issues became a part of the U.S. government's reasons for the Troubled Asset Relief Program (TARP), but this supportive appropriation of slightly more than $700 billion dollars is to only cover some of the largest American corporations. This becomes a factor of how larger businesses could restructure, but a vast amount of smaller businesses failed, and went out of business. American International Group (AIG) was factored in this concern even as they provided insurance underwriting support for thousands of other smaller independent insurance businesses. Some of these insurance companies have different corporate names, but they are subsidiary offices throughout the United States, and in other countries that AIG has underwritten agreements with. Therefore this is part of why the U.S. government considered a bailout agreement for various businesses including AIG, General Motors (GM), Chrysler, and various banks to outline that they were "too big and important" to a vast amount of people, and businesses to fail.

Observing how most of these conflicts within AIG, GM, and Chrysler exist within business, and corporate corrections becomes another value which has started with mergers, and corporate or business buyouts with some transactions by government. General Motors restructured after a month in bankruptcy during 2009, and they eliminated Oldsmobile, and the Saturn Corporation in 2010. Chrysler Corporation filed bankruptcy, and then accepted major ownership from Fiat with them gaining over 50% of its controlling interest in of the company. The strongest conflicting "merger, and acquisitions" that were recommended, and supported from government stem from the troubled CEO Robert Willemstad's tenure at AIG. He was replaced by Edward Liddy as CEO, and along with other companies they became truly worth less with other issues of how they were surviving throughout the better U.S. economic times with productive earnings. Apart from all three of these corporations AIG was the most complex corporate business that had to sell off various corporate subsidiary businesses. AIG also consisted of various asset management divisions, and business group issues that have been considered for negotiated sale of these divisions, and asset holdings.

AIG's massive business structure observing a need for mergers, and acquisition concerns consisted of foreign and domestic businesses. Considering AIG was started in Shanghai, China in 1919 by an American named Cornelius Starr selling the Chinese people insurance, this business grew between America, China, and other countries. Today the company expanded with its headquarters located in New York, and they have thousands of offices, and affiliate insurance companies that manage their insurance underwritten agreements. Their most vital transactions have started with Pacific Century Group in 2009 whom is an Asia based company that bought out AIG's subsidiary of Pine Bridge Investments.

During 2009 AIG also sold its Colombia business operation to Ecuador's Blanco Del Pichincha. Prudential Insurance Co had offered negotiation's to buy an Asian operation owned by AIG named; American International Assurance (AIA) for $30.5 to $35.5 billion dollars, but AIG did not won't to except nothing but the price of $35.5 billion dollars. Apart from that, Prudential and its shareholders reconsidered their bid not to go pass the $30.5 billion dollar mark which they had reconsidered after their 1st bid at $35.5 billion dollars. In March 2010 AIG agreed to sell its American Life Insurance Co. (Alico) to MetLife Inc. for $15.5 billion dollars, and this business consisted of annuities, life, and health insurance in various places throughout the world. Also this agreement made AIG the 2nd largest shareholder of MetLife Inc. with a stake of more than 20% ownership in the MetLife Company.

Another AIG issue to pay-off the U.S. government bailout loan existed when AIG agreed to sale two of their foreign subsidiary businesses consisting of life insurance companies. These AIG subsidiary's in Japan named AIG Star and AIG Edison were part of an agreement to be sold to Prudential for a price of $4.2 billion dollars in cash, and $600 million in assumed third party debt to the U.S. government. From the sale of Alico, and an initial public offering for AIA, and the spin-off of an AIG aircraft leasing company "International Lease Fiancés Corporation", this also consisted of another initial public offering. The company AIG, and these spin off businesses have made it possible to be able to pay tens of billions of dollars back to the U.S. government, and operate (c/o insurance clams) with salaries for their employees. This, and other issues was outlined to the U.S. Federal Reserve Bank of New York credit facility to make payments during 2010 with the CEO Bob Benmosche, and Chairman Robert Miller of AIG managing these, and other transactions. These AIG transactions have accomplished a recovery of over $36 billion dollars within U.S. government bailout agreements. This format of transactions was factually important to raise funds that were payable for their U.S. government bailout requirements.

One of the largest factors that made thousands of local, and commerce banks including some insurance companies being affiliated with "AIG" junk bond rated issues was the severe result of credit defaults, foreclosures, and unemployment. These problems became worse due to an increase in bankruptcies within companies such as Wachovia, Countrywide, Washington Mutual, Bear Stearns, Lehman Brothers, and a vast amount of others. Observing this the U.S. banking industry was a factor that caused extensive problems with Fannie Mae, and Freddie Mac which had accumulated bad loans for years before 2008. These two Government Sponsored Enterprise's which became a problem within the "sub-prime lending mortgage market caused a crisis" with them becoming insolvent before restructuring. This conditional resource within Fannie Mae, and Freddie Mac consisted of their involvement with investment banks offering Credit Default Swaps, and Mortgage Backed Securities. Then these commercial banks suffered from these loans that were originally established at their bank business offices. Therefore the level of failure, and financial losses occurred throughout investment banks, local banks, mortgage lenders, and others including the American system of government. The American society of business, and the level of social justice concerning these factors will take years if not decades to correct.

This business progress of corrections has been pursued with the junk bond rating, and the takeover of Countrywide whom was bought out by Bank of America. During 2008 Bank of America purchased the Countrywide Financial institution for $4.1 billion dollars upon which a serious concern was outlined from the U.S. Congress, and regulators in the federal government. Countrywide Financial, and their board Chairman and CEO Angelo Mozilo observed this conflict within financial disasters years before. Even the observed concern to recognize how the state of California allowed Enron to manipulate their energy market, this was the same conflict with Countrywide, but their manipulation was throughout the American housing mortgage market. Therefore considering this conflict occurred at Bank of America whom also received U.S. government TARP bailout money, their CEO Ken Lewis was criticized and removed from his position of leadership. This action occurred due to his companies' involvement in this corporate buyout with government money.

Washington Mutual Inc. became another large banking business with tremendous losses that were conflicting with 29 corporate acquisitions from 1990 to 2006. This conditionally was a strong issue of were a business had purchased more banking establishments then the company could handle, especially when a mortgage crisis was lingering. During September of 2008 the United States Office of Thrift Supervision (OTS) seized Washington Mutual Bank from Washington Mutual Incorporated, and placed it into receivership under the Federal Deposit Insurance Corporation's (FDIC) jurisdiction. No more than a year later the FDIC sold the banking subsidiary to J.P. Morgan Chase for $1.9 billion dollars, and this included legal arguments from Washington Mutual Inc. in the courts. Considering the conditions under the Federal Deposit Insurance Corporation jurisdiction, various activities are a vital consideration of bank, business, government, and personal economic survival.

The observation of Washington Mutual Bank was targeted due to a withdrawal of $16.4 billion dollars, and therefore the sale of this company to J.P. Morgan Chase by the FDIC was discretionary, and then additional negotiations had to be considered. This was part of the crisis in the U.S. banking industry, and therefore this transaction was approved "minus the unsecured debt or equity clams" that existed. A high rate of credit defaults, and debt was factual within taking this under consideration for the liquidity requirements by the Bank Holding Company Act, and the FDIC.

After the 2008 failure of Washington Mutual Bank the 4ᵗʰ largest bank in America, Wachovia had purchased a vast amount of banking establishments, merged with some insurance company business issues, and then failed to observe certain bad asset holdings of their business purchases. After deregulation of the Glass Steagall Act, and the misconception of other laws a vast amount of banks, and insurance companies took full advantage of the economic and financial values that existed. This became conditional throughout the United States with Wachovia being one of the many aggressive participants. Wachovia was established in 1908 with its headquarters in Charlotte, North Carolina, and in 2001 Wachovia Securities and

Prudential Securities Inc. (c/o Prudential Financial Inc.) agreed on a merger to become Wachovia Securities LLC.

Observing the year 2003 Wachovia acquired Metropolitan West Securities, and in 2005 they lost a bid for MBNA, but later that year they bought Westcorp which increased their banking presence in the southern region of California. In 2006 Wachovia agreed to purchase Golden West Financial with their commercial bank branches named World Savings Bank for $25.5 billion dollars that gave them even more of the California market, and additional bank branches in a vast amount of other states. Then during May of 2007 Wachovia bought out AG Edwards for $6.8 billion dollars to make them the 2nd largest retail broker in the United States with 16,000 brokers through their subsidiary Wachovia Securities. This format of banking, insurance, and investment banking is something that was slightly forbidden after the Glass Steagall Act was established as law in the 1930s up until the disastrous repeal during 1999 of the Glass Steagall Act regulation.

The California and Arizona housing market became severely bad off, and with a few other economic hard knocks such as a California energy crisis which Enron Corp also took billions from California was part of a long-term regional economic problem. With newly retired citizens considering a second home in Arizona, California, Florida, and a few other states, this consisted of hundreds of thousands of people that had to reconsider, or give up the additional home they have. Then they had to make this decision, and evaluation due to the conditions of banks, various bankrupt financial institutions, and businesses that destroyed their retirement savings. This included Wachovia Bank which became part of this complex economic equation, and crisis. Considering defaulted lending, and severe damage to the mortgage backed securities market with other conflicts this was the accumulation of strikes against Wachovia, and their CEO Robert Steel which included investors, and depository customers.

Contrary to California's problems that would soon become an issue of if the state would file for bankruptcy, Wachovia had established a massive corporate structure spanning throughout most parts of California, and the United States. This tremendous corporate business structure caused various businesses to become questionable, and this was even more factual with an overbuilt real estate market of attractive commercial, and residential facilities that could not be sold fast enough to make a profit. When the financial crisis hit in 2007, and more so 2008 Wachovia like other banking institutions was being hit hard with losses in the billions of dollars. Wachovia's issues of debt had reached $191 billion dollars, and the federal government owned $39 billion dollars of that concern. Therefore this means that it would cost the FDIC too much to insure a failure on their deposits which was comparable at hundreds of other banks.

Wachovia became an issue of whom would the FDIC (c/o the SEC) allow to buyout the entire business operation of Wachovia bank. The two likely choices who had interest in buying the company was Citigroup, and Wells Fargo. The FDIC and their Chairwoman Sheila Bair, the Officer of Thrift Supervision (OTS) Director John Reich, the Office of the Comptroller of the Currency, the IRS, and other federal government officials had involvement in this matter due to the possible price that this would cost the U.S. government.

Observing the extensive problem at Wachovia, this and other transactions would cost the U.S. government billions of dollars, contrary to the billions of dollars they have loss in tax revenue from bankrupt businesses. This becomes the process of which company would be productive within the purchase, and manageable control of Wachovia's massive assets, and not deter the $30 to $35 billion dollars that is normally held by the FDIC. Both Wells Fargo, and Citigroup went through a complex level of negotiations with Wachovia, and most all U.S. federal banking regulators to determine the logical bidder. This logical winning bidder consisted of understanding the holding of manageable discipline of Wachovia's commercial real estate holdings. Also these values included how the future of Wachovia, and others would be able to lend money to households, and businesses to keep a strong economy in America.

In September 2008 day by day negotiations became tremendous between both Wells Fargo, and Citigroup coming together at the table to understand if a deal could be approved without FDIC assistance.

Contrary to no FDIC assistance Robert Steel and Wachovia invited Wells Fargo and Citigroup to a meeting upon which both had proposals which held predications on the FDIC assistance. Wells Fargo offered to cover the first $2 billion dollars of losses on a pool of $127 billion dollars-worth of assets as well 80% of subsequent losses. This was under the condition of if Wells Fargo with a combined new company would grow large enough to competitively restructure. Then therefore this would cap the FDIC's losses on the first $20 billion dollars, and an additional $4 billion dollars a year for three years.

Understanding that they also agreed on giving the FDIC $12 billion dollars in Wachovia preferred stock, and stock warrants (c/o the rights to buy stock at a predetermined price) as compensation, then the FDIC would cover any additional losses above $42 billion dollars. Substantially this negotiation was the lesson observed from the tremendously bad corporate mergers, and more so buyouts that Wachovia had made a short time before their failure that began in 2007. Considering these facts Wells Fargo, and Citigroup had positioned their strategy not to make the same mistake, and wanted to be dependent on the "Fullest Faith and Credit" of the U.S. government possible. Therefore some will say these businesses within America's banking industry were depending on government money, and assistance similar to welfare, but they are paying large fees to control certain business assets. This level of Corporate Welfare became tremendously complex for thousands of American businesses. Then basically between Wells Fargo, and Citigroup they had recognized how important it was to keep themselves out of receivership, and or bankruptcy for the benefit of expanding their business in a corporate welfare environment.

Observing these negotiations the FDIC board voted to support assistance for Wachovia, and this became a bidding war of diversionary resources. The outrage was with Wells Fargo because Citigroup was chosen as the winner, and then the FDIC signed an agreement in principal. Following that, Wachovia, and Citigroup executed an exclusive technical agreement that prohibited Wachovia from among other things negotiating with other potential acquiring businesses.

This becomes part of a buyout process that can be somewhat expensive, and conflicting. Understanding the midst of the market turmoil, the Federal Open Market Committee (FOMC) met at the end of September 2008, at about the same time they announced the Citigroup acquisition of Wachovia, and the invocation of systemic risk exception.

The planned merger of these 2 very large institutions of Citigroup, and Wachovia led to some concerns from the FOMC participants that the bigger, and increasingly bigger firms that were being created would become "too big to fail". This value of concern was in accordance to a letter from the Federal Reserve Chairman Ben Bernanke to the Federal Crisis Inquire Commission (FCIC) whom was holding concern about the U.S. financial crisis. He added that he shared this concern and voiced hope that TARP would create options other than mergers for managing problems at larger institutions. Then subsequently this concern was outlined through the process of regulation reform. This was the understanding upon which we might develop a good resolution of mechanisms, and decisively address the issue of financial concentration that is applied with too big to fail businesses.

Citigroup and Wachovia immediately began working on the deal; even as Wachovia's stock fell 81.6% to $1.84 on September 29, 2008 which was the day that TARP was initially rejected by Congressional lawmakers. They faced tremendous pressure from the regulators, and the markets to conclude the transaction before the following trading day of Monday, but the deal was viewed as complicated. Citigroup was not acquiring the holding company, just the bank, and Citigroup wanted to change some of the original terms within managing this massive company, and maybe to manage the money better. Then came a surprise on Tuesday morning, October 2, 2008 Wells Fargo returned to the table, and made a competing bid to buy all of Wachovia for $7.00 a share. This was seven times more than Citigroup's bid, with no government assistance. From this point the deal was completed with very little conflicts as Wachovia had been bought out by Wells Fargo after Wachovia barely could hold market value. Observing this large capacity buyout with the survival of banking institutions in America only becoming the largest businesses possible, it is relevant to understand why other businesses have a tremendous time with business survival, or expansion.

Throughout the American society the support for big companies is strangely conflicting to the extent that small businesses operated by American born citizens in becoming a rare value. A vast amount of corporate American businesses have a tremendous amount of smaller locations which on occasions is now taking away from the smaller businesses with good ideas. Most professional offices and businesses still find a way to be productive, but if the Constitution of the state and federal government are not honored or enforced effectively the chance of business survival becomes severely conflicting. These issues very well could be the problem with very large retail, and restaurant chains like Borders Books, Circuit City Electronics, and Bennigan's Restaurants upon who had a large percentage of facilities, and or locations. These multiple amount of corporate locations then became the management's decision to closed during restructuring from their filings of bankruptcy.

These good and bad issues of management become the factor of how a vast amount of government officials will ignore various anti-trust laws, and personal appeal values. The values of concern consist of how some people use defamation of character against the best managers, and the pursuit of the hiring of weaker managers have provided an accumulation of losses. Then these American small business owners or corporate owned small business facilities have a lack of discipline to compete against other businesses upon which some are becoming foreign owned businesses. Then we recognize why most small banking establishments apart from Wells Fargo, Citigroup, Bank of America, and others whom have become the strong survivors have issue to control most industry conditions of business.

To regain vital industry standards the mind set of values within state and federal Constitutional laws must be stood firmly on which the courts truly must support the effort of an individual or business as it applies to the people. Then this becomes their ambition for productive business ownership. Contrary to the notion that too big to fail, and programs like TARP that puts larger businesses back in order with additional lending contrary to their good, and bad issues of management this equation must improve. This becomes the problem with U.S. government agencies that local government and others take for granted. These issues vitally include how the U.S. Post Office (c/o 2010) is running out of money, and government funds at (FEMA) the Federal Emergency Management Agency due to an enormous amount of disasters is spending too much money. Upon this understanding the real factor is that on occasions some businesses are being bought up with issues of expansion of being too complex. Then the backwards motion of the American society of business exist within the compound of business that clams not to worry until management or even labor takes severe losses with companies moving out of the country. Therefore a junk bond can be found in a large or small company capacity especially when conflicting issues are used to manipulate the true progress within expansion of small productive business.

CHAPTER NINE
JUNK BOND MARKETS OUT OF CONTROL

IIIIIIIIIIIIIIIIIIIIIIIIIIIIIIIIIIIIIIIIIIIIIIIIIIIIIIIIIIIIIIIIII

The American junk bond issues within the U.S. financial markets has been a tremendous concern for orderly business during the 1990s, and the 1st decade of the 2000s. Junk bond issues within corporate business have occasionally been high yielding, and risky investments with value that outline various economic, and financial concerns of a corporate business. These issues of good and more so lately bad resources of corporate transactions are part of a discipline that has reduced the amount of businesses in America. Contrary to tremendous problems in the banking industry, various transportation, and oil companies like United Continental Holding Inc., ConocoPhillips Company, and ExxonMobil Corporation just to name a few, created mergers to better survive. If the massive oil companies had to do this to restructure, the transportation airline companies, and others like banks have vital restructuring with similar concerns in this conflicting business environment of a "severely or conditionally" bad economy.

Before the merger of United Airlines Inc., and Continental Airlines the U.S. airline industry suffered very expensive problems such as the September (9-11 Report) terrorist attacks. These terrorist attacks cost United Airlines Inc. billions of dollars in assets, employees, and a tremendous loss of revenue which was similar to other industry market business disasters. Also before the Exxon Corporation and

Mobil Oil Corporation merged various severe accidents caused a vast amount of diversified problems. This became part of a very expensive corporate level of damages between their business operation, the victim/plaintiff, and the U.S. government. The severe liability of this problem occurred with the Exxon Corporation, Amoco Oil Corporation, and a few other chemical companies.

The Exxon Valdez oil tanker spill in 1989 caused a severe problem in the Alaskan Bay, and cost Exxon Corporation hundreds of millions of dollars. This level of negligence also disrupted distribution, slowed down expensive offshore oil drilling operations, and then nearly rated them as a junk bond issue for a brief duration of time. The business within Conoco Inc., and Phillips Petroleum Company consisting of a merger was a mix of complacent business disciplines, and junk bond rated business values. Phillips Petroleum Co. was the consideration of a junk bond issue by T-Boone Pickens whom made an unsuccessful hostile takeover attempt to purchase the company. Conoco Inc. had different concerns with large investments, and takeover concerns from the Seagram Company while Phillips Petroleum Company was supporting a white knight partner issue with the DuPont Company from certain corporate raiders.

A vast amount of junk bond issues were created due to certain accidents in chemical refineries, and manufactures with some corporate businesses suffering through conflicting problems during the 1990s, and 2000s. These conflicts including issues within "business/industry disasters, and terrorist attacks" which became very expensive are a vital American concern that must be dealt with in a logical way. This severely expense business, and industry condition that carried a high cost to survive in various market industries was an issue that American businesses, people as professionals, and the government needed to control. These were similar factors throughout the American Steel industry, the U.S. Transportation Airline industry, some automotive service businesses (c/o cabs and buses), and oil companies with competitive industry concerns of restructuring. This becomes the observation of small independent business operations that are sometimes closely associated with large companies. These troubled small and large business losses also included government investment municipal bonds being downgraded within the cities, and towns which these businesses existed, and operated with or even within franchise issues of management. Also within these resources of business that must be considered in the right capacity of junk bond purchase procedures, the concept of corporate control becomes a vital responsibility.

Understanding certain catastrophic vital issues the American society of industry standards within engineering, and industrial processes must improve so that these conflicts are not the only reasons that become important for businesses to be involved in a merger, and or be bought out. American standards, national security, and legislature with deregulation are some of the conflicts that have instigated a devaluation of various businesses in America. An observation of corporate conflicts with certain levels of complacent management, or misguided labor union issues as it applies to companies like Exxon, Amoco, or even MCI's survival have an array of issues that is conflicting with secured business. Then these are the true condition of factual relevance that caused these companies to be rated as a junk bond issue. Observing this, the publicly held corporations with a good set of board of directors, and various employees (contrary to family ownership) are usually the beneficiary. Therefore if they lose business interest, or they don't make the best business decisions, this is when the company may be better off in a merger, or be active in the process of being bought out.

These issues of transition become a normal condition of people buying a person's business, or a corporation (c/o merger or buyout activity) that usually has a logic with investing in something that can be beneficial. These beneficial factors have a logic which is also part of good managing duties. Then, these are factors within earning money which includes providing a service or various products in a business capacity to have a logical increase of value. The observation of these values even may include when management changes occur.

Between 2008 thru 2011 the American banking industry has had the most management changes with corporate buyouts recommended by government, and with expectations of better resource values. Within the same condition of concern these are values established from the board of directors or the format of upper management with the determination to have certain well operated corporations that will take logical control of failing business operations. These changes that occur are important for the reason of more productive people replacing other employees that were sometimes complacent, and nonproductive. Therefore, if "management was right" with these transactions of concern, and other values appropriating law in America, junk bond restructuring issues, and other market business matters can come together with levels of progress. Then considering this, these are the levels of progress that benefit American businesses, and the logic of the American society with conditions of improvements that were needed.

The term "Junk Bond" applies to publicly traded companies that have a questionable future within being a long term stable company that might fit better as a subsidiary of a well operated, and financially disciplined company of value. Some corporate raiders like T-Boone Pickens, Carl Icahn, the late Reginald Lewis, and others like Ted Turner have created businesses, and various liquidity values of expansion in these selective business dealings. Throughout the United States other conditions of business have existed within occasions of people taking unlawful advantage of corporate funded business transactions similar to investment banker Bernard Madoff, and Bernard Ebbers of WorldCom Corporation. Their process of making money, and then severely losing money with certain unlawful disciplines was a tremendous problem. These transactions are considered with various illogical conflicts of business interest similar to insider trading that where not lawfully pursued until damage was severely observed.

Considering bad corporate junk bond rated businesses have been taken apart, and then a larger business is prosecuted to the extent that any supportive or smaller business has been put into a manipulated direction, this is a problem that gives a regional economy need for overall restructuring. Observing this, the concept of an established business has been diverted out of its original intent, which makes restructuring vital. The critical example was the Enron Corporation purchase, and control of Portland GE where this public utility companies employees had all of their invested pension savings at stake. Then within these business valued efforts which have severely been rearranged, most business conditions had to be restructured if the business was to ever exist again. Upon this observation Portland GE was a public utility company in Portland, Oregon that the majority of those citizens depend on as a logical monopoly, and therefore their existence is slightly inevitable. Contrary to the fact this observation sometimes means the business has been sold, and then put into a conditional value of restructuring from its unworkable business operation of standards that must be corrected.

As we observe a junk bond market that is out of control, Americans find a vast amount of corporate and private businesses such as banking establishments going into various diversified economic directions. Observing the economic crisis of 2008 in the month of October the United States government created the Troubled Asset Relief Program (TARP) which was to bailout certain banks, and some businesses from economic distress. These conflicting directions by the economy, and some of the largest businesses in America consisted of newly developed problems that were not always a forward motion of progress. This economic downfall is due to a lack of full sovereignty, and destructive business decisions that the American system of banking, and government had not prevented so well over the years.

The concept of banking that was deregulated throughout the years of 1998 to 2012 has been part of bank businesses like Indy Mac Bank, Countrywide Financial, Washington Mutual, and Wachovia Bank that became industry losses as junk bond issues. These losses were accumulated after the repeal of the Glass Steagall Act, which gave them additional conflicting assets in America's largest investment banks, and commerce banks. The increase of assets within U.S. banks such as Bank of America, Citigroup, J.P. Morgan, Wachovia, and Wells Fargo went from $2.2 trillion to $6.8 trillion dollars of bank assets between 1998 to 2007 with this legislative conflict. From there, these values in 2008 were part of businesses, and a certain amount of American households that became part of an economic system that loss somewhere over $11 trillion dollars in the mortgage, and credit crisis with extensive negative results.

Countrywide was the largest mortgage lender in the United States to fail in the late 2000s decade. They caused suffering that can be considered as a bad or inappropriate corporate citizen that has pushed the America society backwards. Countrywide Financial became a junk bond issue that was bought out by Bank of America for a price of $4.1 billion dollars. In the same conflicting concern the investment bank of Merrill Lynch also suffered severely, and this was an issue applied to various mortgage lenders, and bank loan clients. Their losses from Mortgage Backed Security investments, and credit defaults became a tremendous problem for Americans that did not have enough money for their obligations, or that did not manage their money properly. From there Merrill Lynch was also bought out by Bank of America which was conflicting due to Bank of America receiving TARP funds from the U.S. government. These were the conflicting decisions that financial bankers, and the American system of government made with conditional negative results (c/o the Glass Steagall Act. Repeal) which also led to other banking failures. The investment bank Bear Stearns was the next failure, and then they were bought out by J.P. Morgan Chase. After the 1930s these buyouts with a commercial bank owning an investment bank were slightly or conditionally forbidden by law.

Washington Mutual and Wachovia Bank became some of the other more discretionary junk bond issues within publicly owned banking, and financial companies during 2007, and 2008. This becomes the factor throughout the banking industry were business control had to be reestablished by government, and corporate conditions of restructuring. Washington Mutual became a business upon which they also loss heavily within these credit market sectors, and then they were advised by the U.S. government to expect a buyout offer from J.P. Morgan Chase. Wachovia Bank was the fourth largest bank in the United States before they became a junk bond issue during 2007, and 2008.

Wells Fargo bought out Wachovia which included all of the other financial businesses that Wachovia had purchased, and this addition made Wells Fargo one of the largest retail bank-brokers in the United States. This fast turnover within losses of assets was tremendous due to their exclusive acquisitions between 2001, and 2006 upon which then in 2007 and 2008 they had to be bought out as a "rescue". Indy Mac Bank was left with the same conflict upon which they had been directed to the control of the IMB Holdings business issue which considered that Indy Mac Bank had a bit over $13.5 billion dollars in assets. Then there was the Lehman Brothers banking company who was sold off after their bankruptcy filing. The purchase of Lehman Brothers consisted of a sale of 1 part of the business being sold to Barclays of the United Kingdom, and another half being sold to Nomure Holdings of Japan. This left Lehman Brothers Inc. in a position of whom under certain laws had property issues that were an ownership purchase concern against certain issued negotiations with the Goldman Sachs Group.

With American banks filing for bankruptcy a certain amount of other problems included foreign businesses taking over the controlling values of American establishments of business. American bank business clients like Inland Steel becoming ArcelorMittal Steel, Amoco Oil becoming BP, and Zenith Corp becoming LG Electronics has shifted economic, and financial values in various banking directions. Understanding this, various foreign businesses also have a tendency not to honor the U.S Constitution that gives all logical, and law binding citizens various opportunities. These are conflicting, and or unlawful values that were not being considered on the new foreign business owners list of valued disciplines. This is observed without U.S corporate citizen responsibilities, and various social concerns including the relocating of their corporate headquarters. Therefore this truly is a problem that the U.S. government, and some state governments have allowed without enforceable corrections in a timely manner.

Some black American communities near, or in big cities as it applies to business have been hit worse than some rural white country towns that may consist of farming or coal mining industry values of condition. Black Americans have slightly moved ahead in some ways, but how the black community works together includes the understanding of the good, and bad of white Americans. This observation is based on the values of business and government being managed by productive black Americans. An enormous conflict also includes black Americans in the upper levels of corporate management that have ignored certain black American social values that must improve. This becomes the troubling factors of when black American businesspeople cannot achieve business levels of prosperity to eliminate various issues of gang violence, and corruption throughout their communities, and government.

Another tremendous problem exists within black American Muslims that have acted inappropriately to the extent of supporting various Middle East enemy foreign agendas. Even during the election victory of President Barack Obama these same black "panther party" Muslims threatened white Americans in a few locations throughout New York. This truly is a destructive problem for the American society of people. Also this is only a slight diversion from the activity of the Ku Klux Klan (KKK) being destructive, and violent against black Americans, and others including various decent white Americans. The distraction of this is a vital concern with whites, and more so black Americans working, and making the effort together to outline a better capacity of discipline, and togetherness as Americans. These good and conditionally bad issues of working together throughout America also applies too not supporting gang violence, or various enemy foreign agenda's upon which have been the losing objective of certain businesses, and good and bad organizations. Reginald Lewis understood this factor well by being lawfully aggressive in business, but also working with all nationality types of Americans to achieve his business goals.

Beatrice International was a company that operated worldwide, and therefore it consisted of various challenges for Reginald Lewis, and the company. These were challenges that are found in America, and also in countries that are not governed as well as the United States. A vast amount of these other countries sometimes consist of a total lack of domestic tranquility, and this keeps them from being actively part of an established, and well-developed society. Even how companies like Beatrice International may help provide humanitarian efforts with other conditions of business disciplines becomes a factor of having a workable understanding of other cultural values. This can be applicable with the respect of how people work, and live as it applies to American values. Therefore considering him buying into a large corporation like Beatrice International Foods his duty as Chairman and CEO meant that all employees, and assets must have workable components to restructure a company that was rated as a junk bond issue. Observing Beatrice International, this was the second company that Reginald Lewis worked to buyout, and restructure before his untimely death. Then this became discretionary to most values within business expansion with timing to achieve progress that could not be managed or established with increasing economic values.

Contrary to nationality issues, a tremendous problem is observed were large corporations, and individuals will take advantage of small businesses, and sometimes that includes all kinds of investors. Some WorldCom, and MCI merger, and or buyout concerns more so consisted of issues that have offered an array of problems within small companies expanding. This was conflicting to the American society of businesses upon which this reduces the amount of new U.S. businesses (c/o nonprofessional) establishments. Observing this between 1990 and 2011 American businesses including individuals as professionals have loss investment dollars, and on occasions accountable business earnings. Bernard Ebbers of the WorldCom Corporation was one of the most conflicting businesspeople that took advantage of smaller businesses which included violating U.S. Anti-Trust laws. Considering this with them as a telecommunications company, various smaller businesses were threatened with conflicting debt, or they suffered severe issues of business survival.

A stronger part of business conflicts within evidence was how Bernard Ebbers fell far behind in margin call investment accounts which consisted of his stock sales. These sales of stock within him owning WorldCom stock with a large fiduciary capacity of holdings displayed a lack of lawful trust. He then needed to cover $400 million dollars in margin losses while WorldCom's stock in 2000 was losing tremendously before bankruptcy. Between 1990, and up to the year 2010 Bernard Madoff, and even William Daly in 1991 to 2001 caused investors to lose from previous junk bond issues that controlled various corporate assets. These were businesses that Americans depend on within services, and or contract disciplines of employment which lately during 2011 have severely suffered. William Daly, and Ameritech Corp violated Anti-Trust laws tremendously that manipulated small American businesses, and supported an enemy foreign agenda. This was conditional with Middle Eastern people between Indiana and Illinois benefiting from these severe problems to America, and certain conflicts within small, and large businesses. Then we as Americans, and or professionals had to endure the understanding that small investors are losing substantially more than most logical citizens. This even included some small businesses whom suffered losses from larger businesses going into bankruptcy, and laying off employees. Therefore small investors that owned a small business were pushed fare back or out of business apart from businesses that sold an important group of commodities (c/o some Hedge Funds) such as within oil, gas, and or food.

The safest businesses economically, and most times being productive with involvement in the "recent" corporate merger, and or buyout process within junk bond issues were by various U.S. defense contractors. The productive history within General Electric Corporation, Raytheon Corporation, and General Dynamics pursuing the buyout of various businesses, and defense product divisions is part of a workable format. This logical format of business is part of them being astute within government business procedures. Even Motorola Inc, and their business agreements with General Dynamics had been conducted by this format of business in a capacity which they usually have positive government intervention.

On some occasions various corporate business defense contract agreements with certain products have a priority which means they may be working conditionally close, or closer than other businesses, and people to government which most times have factored a loss of value. This is the understanding upon which these are sometimes unlawful opinions, and conflicts that are important, but it is vital for them to manage good workable values together. These are conflicting values that most American businesses are considering within the logic of improving earnings that have been the result of a vast amount of corporate mergers. Understanding those earnings they usually effect a vast amount of most households, the establishments of church, some schools, and other active and helpful establishments that receive contributions and support. Therefore how defense contractors argue, and support various establishments becomes a legal condition that on occasions have been factually a threat with trust busting.

The format of values within trust busting consist of U.S. Anti-Trust law issues with conflicts that hold business, and individuals occasionally back are conditional problems with a loss of productive resources. This concept of manipulation is truly bad! Considering this the company or business owner then dose not "seem" to be dependable which becomes a serious problem. Understanding these conditions of trust, and trust busting with various "conflict personal values" of importance can distort someone's true ability to be productive in business, and society.

Observing these U.S. Anti-Trust issues of confidence between people like Bernard Madoff, and his Ponzi scheme which included various bad corporate transactions, or sometimes no transactions at all when excepting investment money certain American investors were provided a large loss. This has made the U.S. economy tremendously complex to restructure with a vast amount of investors that loss their life savings. Even companies such as WorldCom, and more so Ameritech whom had a tremendous conflicting effect on the America economy has caused negative repercussions to the valued conditions of the American economy. Trust-busting at these levels is a loss of trustworthy values were lawful managing is destroyed from various bad investments, and business concerns. These factors exist more so for the courts to decide on, and then the consideration of merger and buyout activities where business can expand, or government tax revenue can be logical and effective a resolution is provided.

Various criminal issues of corporate business concerns with junk bond factors accumulate the factual problem of not allowing certain progress to occur. This is tremendously unworkable for businesses in the American society. Upon close observation this vitally includes values within investors or citizens involved in business to achieve their most logical conditions of prosperity. Lately this has also included sometimes people supporting an enemy foreign agenda. Upon these factors a newly started business may ruin themselves, and other businesspeople involved in the process of business ownership planning. These levels of harm in American industry during 1998 to 2010 have consisted of massive activity within junk bond buyout, and merger conditions that were arbitrary conditions of business. This has been observed in the American banking industry, and more so within the internet computer companies that experienced an expanding sector of business during the 1990s. AOL and their subsidiary Netscape, the Microsoft Corp, Apple Inc, Yahoo, Goggle, and others which were businesses that became part of this trend of technology failures, and success are valuable assets to the American society. When the banking industry, and these U.S. internet business issues of concern are put together with deregulated financial transactions, some social issues of disaster are almost 100% relevant to occur.

The issue of junk bonds, and some Americans indirectly supporting an enemy foreign agenda has been a conflict with tremendous issues for American social values, government, and especially business. A vast amount of these conditional issues are held with various Americans from a valued life of prosperity, and hopefully the best decisions in business. This also includes how America, and issues of professionalism have hit a record low rate with various industry disciplines similar to junk bond ratings. The American oil industry, the Enron Corporate conflict, the WorldCom Corporate conflict, Hurricane Katrina, and the September 11, 2001 attacks is part of this evidence. These were factual problems within a vast amount of American businesspeople, and government that did not take appropriate alert, and preventative observation.

Before these attacks against the American society of citizens, various foreign people somewhat connected to oil rich countries were all over America supporting conflicts against Americans, and buying most small businesses like gas stations in certain regions. Even the concept of U.S. Anti-Trust laws have become a tremendous factor with illegal monopolies of gas stations that were starting to be an important issue of concern. Within these businesses being controlled by foreign people from the Middle East, and them severely outnumbering American born business owners the effect is almost becoming as bad as the Great Depression days of the 1920s. Contrary to the Great Depression the 2011, and 2012 market for gas has become similar to the way Muammar Gaddafi in the late 1980s manipulated the cost of a barrel of oil. That price for oil would go from $3 dollars a barrel to $30 dollars a barrel in the course of a day, therefore some parts of a recession may have come from foreign controlled business.

Observing the Great Depression of the 1920s, and how a corporation during 2012 is part of the American economy, technology, and corporate buyout issues has become a different atmosphere. This was part of the concern that has tremendous factors with illegal monopolies of gas stations that were starting to be an issue. Within these businesses being controlled by foreign people from the Middle East, and them severely outnumbering American born business owners the effect is tremendous with them illegally owning these businesses directly across the street from each other. The effect of these people sending money out of the United States is unlike more money being invested in other U.S. businesses, and community concerns, but more so with them supporting this Middle Eastern war against America. So considering there was a war before 1920 this almost became as bad as the Great Depression days of the 1920s and 1930s with people that don't care for additional values of American prosperity.

Another important comparison that is applicable to the Great Depression is the financial markets of today that consist of more controlled technology which is a divisive issue, and process that only somewhat manages volatility, but bad investments still exist. Within the logical help of the Securities and Exchange Commission (SEC), the corporate merger/buyout process is governed for most lawful business responsibilities. Now one of the only other considerations becomes how the U.S. Anti-Trust laws are conditionally enforced as some American's observe the values of business ownership, and expansion. The Enron Corporation, WorldCom Corporation, and Ameritech Corporation have put a great amount of American people out of a job, or a business. They have done this within the capacity of violating SEC rules, U.S. Anti-Trust laws, and other issues that supported crimes within advanced issues of technology.

After Ameritech Corp, WorldCom Corp, and Enron Corporation committed destructive crimes against various American citizens, this and other values became part of the process of certain buyouts that did not seem to hold ground within being a restructured, or a well-established business. This issue and problem has established one-third of the economic problems of the American economy. Another one-third was due to the mortgage crisis, and various catastrophic events upon which society was factored with a new course of technological values which were not considered or managed well enough. Ameritech Corporation (c/o AT&T) operated for less than 10 years, and by doing business as a regional monopoly (c/o residential & commercial customers) they were able to manipulate enormous amounts of people, and instigate conflicting opinions. Contrary to gang violence, and prostitution Ameritech also supported enemy foreign agendas by eliminating various American born business owners. This was done with the help of William Daly, and a few others throughout Chicago, and Northwest Indiana. His observation, and effort to commit defamation of character against certain small investors even included some support from black fraternities that did not have good intentions.

You can also recognize this within the amount of schools that have closed due to students, and teachers who had an inappropriate attitude which was totally indifferent from some of the better people in government, and business. At the same time, places like Chicago, Detroit, Los Angles, New Orleans, and more so Gary, Indiana became labeled as murder "Capitals"! Therefore this caused a vast amount of small businesses to be misguided, and also government municipal bonds to be headed towards being rated at junk bond levels of value. This was due to government also not having productive people managed properly including their severe trouble of enforcing various laws.

Ameritech Corporation became an issue of business as a public company that was nearly rated as "junk", but AT&T was their lifeline to be protected, sold off, bought out, and or controlled with discipline. AT&T in this concern was a parent company for Ameritech, and a vast amount of businesses that they have started, or that they acquired over the decades. Even more so during the 1990s and 2000s within merger or buyout activity in America this was part of their competitive values of business. This may also look like a Junk Bond constituent that has some values of being out of control, but they are one of the major U.S. monopolies with extensive values of resourceful divesture. The concept of divesture is part of certain large corporations that have some obsolete or outdated products, and or equipment which in business consist of asset liability, and legal concerns. Then the other part of divesture is the consolidation of good, and bad business issues to be restructured within research. Various issues of research, and development with business consist of conditions of mergers, and or acquisitions including future conditions in business that will materialize. Therefore observing AT&T they are a strong company with valid liquidity to acquire businesses upon which they can use to create a higher level of business activity. This then becomes a contingent liability factor to keep up with the wired, and wireless telecommunication industry, and certain competitors without being rated as a junk bond.

Other corporations that have been involved in the corporate merger or buyout process are making conditionally small steps (c/o positive & negative results) within the likes of effort within the Sprint-Nextel Corporation. The merger of Sprint Corporation, and their CEO's Daniel Hesse which he was preceded by Gary Foresee a former CEO, and Nextel Corporation with their CEO Tim Donahue gave both companies the opportunity to become the 3rd largest wireless telecommunications company in America. This was part of their hard working, and harsh decisions observing the arbitrary expansion within the format of this agreed merger during 2004. Observing this merger various business issues changed with Sprint and Nextel having a combined merger, and business plan.

Understanding the Sprint and Nextel combination merger creating the Sprint-Nextel Corporation has been a conditional step-by-step issue of achievements. This became the market value of concern similar to others from their decisions in 2011 with Sprint-Nextel Corp buying 30 million iPhones from Apple Inc to give millions of customers a product, and communication service that is in demand. This is an evaluation process to increase their customer base which has been steady with over 50 million subscribers existing from at least the year of 2009. The observation of determination consisted of these two companies becoming one company (Sprint-Nextel Corp), and then they became stronger competitors against AT&T, and Verizon Communications. These are sectored public company businesses that could only maintain their strongest resource of market stability with wired, and wireless telecommunication products, and services.

This aggressive process within businesses involved in a corporate merger concept of activity has given some American corporations additional liquidity, and sometimes valued levels of expansion. During the late 1980s Sprint Corporation was a long distance telephone company, but they had to change with the times, and technology. Sprint Corporation between their 2 CEO's Gary Foresee, and Daniel Hesse managed more than 11 mergers, and acquisitions from 2005 to 2010 during the Sprint-Nextel merger concept of agreements. This was pursued in order for the Sprint-Nextel Corp to discipline, and outline some of its opposition by affiliates which they were forced to initiate discussions of either acquiring some of their affiliates, or to renegotiate the existing agreements. On occasions this becomes common when the affiliates have issues opposing to the merger, and therefore with this process most times they will agree to drop their opposition to a merger. Now up to the changing times during the year of 2011 them, and others like Eastman Kodak have had to endure these similar business issues that only somewhat became workable within business divesture, and restructuring.

During 1994 Eastman Kodak's chemicals subsidiary became a spin off business issue with its own headquarters in the state of Tennessee, contrary to their Rochester, New York headquarters.

The founder George Eastman spent decades after the 1920s with experimentation, and development of certain chemicals in Kingston, Tennessee. This chemical production site during World War II also developed certain explosives for the U.S. Department of Defense which was observed with the Manhattan Project. Upon this format of business restructuring the parent company within Eastman Kodak film products have suffered tremendously. These Eastman companies value of expanded business, and liquidity have been part of conditional progress. Therefore within long term corporate American capitalism, these issues of transition are conditionally made for careful decisions of progress which may include business expansion.

The comparison of Sprint Corporation, Nextel Corporation, Eastern Kodak Corporation, and Sterling Drugs are businesses that had to evaluate various business disciplines. Eastman Kodak Corporation with their buyout of Sterling Drugs (c/o Sterling Winthrop, Inc.) became a vast commitment between film, camera, and now pharmaceutical, and chemical products. Understanding these valued business operations being somewhat a conglomerate for a short or questionable amount of time; the concept of progress goes along the value of business control. Observing this a junk bond issue was created when Eastman Kodak split their company into a spin-off with two parts. One was the film business, and a second was the pharmaceutical and chemical business which has been observed between these business factors, and the original Eastman Kodak Company. Unlike the merger of Sprint-Nextel Corporation, and Eastman Kodak Company which was the major camera, and more so film product resource in America, the changing times have been critical. These are compounded issues from decades ago that have changed with the Eastman Kodak Company from the 1880s, to 2010 with levels of success, and new found conflicting failure. Observing the Sprint-Nextel Corporation they may not ever exceed certain business conditions against AT&T, but they have made some progress with logical profits that keep them in business.

CHAPTER TEN
INTERNATIONAL INVESTMENTS AND INTERNATIONAL TERRORISM

||||||||||||||||||||||||||||||||||||||||||||||||||||||||||||||||

Throughout the American society of business that sometimes includes international issues of business with investments, certain conflicts occurred. This includes conflicting issues of terrorism that are lately becoming issues were small, and some large U.S businesses are being transitioned into foreign ownership. These business societal and U.S. government concerns are values that are a conflict to the overall progress of Americans. Countries without stock exchange's such as Libya, Iraq, Iran, Qatar, Saudi Arabia, Nigeria, and others usually earn a certain amount of wealth as Organization of Petroleum Exporting Countries (OPEC) member throughout a worldwide oil industry. These countries from time to time don't always see eye to eye with American values, therefore them being involved in business in America is seen with certain levels of caution. Observing the issue that they don't have a stock exchange, the corporate merger, and or buyout process vaguely occurs. Considering this factored resource, a transition of secured potential wealth has been accumulated from the large capacity of oil reserves (contrary to investments) that these countries have in common.

The observation of non-OPEC countries may include Japan, Korea, Vietnam, China, the United Kingdom, Germany, and India that do business in America. This is valid with some conditions of business, and people "whom" occasionally don't value the importance of the U.S Constitutional laws. Some of these countries have businesses that have tried to collaborate their corporate business activities that have been used to create markets, and be radical apart from American capitalism, and domestic tranquility. Upon observation, this has been the problem with some American values within the U.S. Constitutional laws, and the rights of citizens being ignored with defamation. Also as a certain amount of misguided Americans have worked to support an enemy foreign agenda, this has victimized other law binding citizens which in a vast amount of the time is connected to business, and certain conditions of economic activity. Therefore the true value of some innocent Americans suffered within their logic to achieve domestic tranquility, with business values, and social levels of prosperity.

Only a fraction of this business process with OPEC nations gives various foreign countries a sense of prosperity. This is the observation, and issue that these nations have as determination, and concern to one day not to just be a trade partner in business, but to establish themselves closer to becoming a well-developed country. If this becomes a corporate American merger, or more so buyout level of effort for their foreign prosperity it hurts the American economy by sending more money, and opportunities overseas. Considering this, the factor of foreign trade concern with other regions of the world must be regulated, and not allowed to abuse U.S. policy values including Constitutional law.

The concept of OPEC, and various diversified product markets are issues within policy values that are sometimes critical within government discussions. The format of these international, and domestic discussions are vital concerns that the United Nations reviews especially following their establishing days in 1945 during Harry Truman's presidential tenure. Most of these issues became a format of American, and international business during the Dwight Eisenhower, and John Kennedy Presidential administrations as international trade became an increasing value, and concern to America. These OPEC countries are also known for having American oil companies in and out of their regions internationally where they earn a certain amount of money from oil, gas, a few other commodities, and business product related items. Also occasionally this includes other American, and international businesses with certain markets upon which these corporate values provide opportunities. Contrary to business, a more vital concern exist within how occasionally some of these countries do conditionally have people that severely support terrorist movements of harm.

The natural resources within oil, gas, and other commodities including technological evaluations are part of what makes American oil companies some of the largest, and most productive in world. This also includes, internet, and wireless telecommunication companies that have worldwide business issues including diversified groups of people that follow certain corporate products like wireless telephones, or computers. Considering this, U.S. businesses somewhat help these other countries, but lately some American businesses have been part of their investments that are more so geared towards businesses with losses that were established in America. As this becomes a conflict for American workers that need various jobs as it applies to the "cost of living", these companies have economic disciplines to be committed too certain values of socially governed justice.

The American steel industry, certain internet companies, and some telecommunication companies have been a vital of part of some foreign business people's concern within venture capital issues. Sense the expanded term of "Global Markets and Global Investments" these factors have become more of an issue, and America has almost suffered into becoming a third world country. These were the issues of American government, and certain businesses that were only prepared to make the best decisions on international business, and markets between America, and other countries.

During the Bill Clinton Presidential administration, and going into the George W Bush 2001 Presidential administration, the U.S. Federal Trade Commission consisted of enormous conflicts. Contrary to some conflicts certain technology business matters which changed for the better conditions of the American society became stronger throughout international, and U.S. domestic markets. This was factual within international and domestic businesspeople whom had a format of doing business in, or with the American society, and sometimes also consolidating their issues of different, and diverse foreign governments. These American's had to be concerned about being able to purchase important products, but also protecting jobs, and managing a level of job security. This was the logic to observe, and accept the fact that the U.S. government was not aware, or was very late within understanding these different social, and economic subjects of harm such as corporate outsourcing to other countries.

Contrary to harmful conflicts, global business from the United States during the 1990s and 2000s has included the activities of corporations such as ExxonMobil Corp, Hess Oil Corp, General Electric Corp, Apple Inc., Microsoft Corp, and others doing well internationally. These are front line companies that should have recognized a vast amount of OPEC, and third world country business issues that have lately consisted of terrorism, and internal war which carries a financial burden, and cost. They did recognize those countries where their work was somewhat lucrative, and evident of radical conflict, but we must have caution with domestic and foreign issues that intervened with the American society. None of these companies being junk bond rated is one reason why these American companies could hold valued business disciplines in these foreign countries.

Besides AT&T, Apple Inc., and Microsoft Corporation being businesses that have appropriated merger, and or buyout competitive expansion issues, other foreign businesses like LG Electronics buying the Zenith Corporation have achieved expansion values. These are companies whom have experimented with manufacturing computers, and telecommunication systems, upon which this being done right becomes a tremendous issue of business, and social evaluations. Also this has left American businesses in a conditional state of being one of very few manufacturing resources of televisions. This became an important business and economic format of logic considering their market values with products held certain levels of progress. These are levels of advancement valuable to American, and international companies. The LG Electronics Company being a South Korean company has maintained extensive manufacturing in South Korea which almost makes them a conglomerate similar to GE Corporation in America.

Contrary to understanding how America would be affected by the September 11, 2001 attacks, and certain foreign businesses taking control of American companies the United States government, and citizens with various local concerns of government at have taken a tremendous loss. Another part of factual issues, and problems is how the loss and gain values of "investments with business growth" is accumulated between good, and bad American issues of foreign policies. The logic of U.S. government policy within Americans for close to a century has been conditionally diversified with issues like U.S. Anti-Trust laws, and trade agreements which includes trade restrictions under certain conditions. Understanding mergers and acquisitions the value of agreements, and foreign relations on trade has been a pivotal factor between various communist countries. These become the values of business, and government in countries that are lawfully regulated with governed, and electoral details.

Understanding various disciplines of government and business which has values similar to well developed countries, this issue of having a logical "Constitution" is a slight diversion from governed societies. Then this includes how a parliament, or a workable format of government usually will keep control of lawful security. A vast amount of business, and employment resources that Americans are losing as opportunities to grow individually in business are the results of these laws not being enforced, or others being deregulated. Considering these factors this is similar to the way Adolph Hitler helped devastate Jews, and other issues that affected the world economy after World War II which left a conflicting future, and economic repercussion following the 1920s.

As America deals with the international problems of Africa, South America, Mexico, the Middle East and others the evaluation of good and bad foreign relations becomes a vital issue to keep terror, and crime at a low to none existent rate on American soil. Mexico with a tremendous illegal drug trade has had issues which includes people being killed on both sides of the Mexican and American border. This is part of a loss within U.S. domestic tranquility in America, and a loss of moral values. Within businesses throughout America that are involved in the corporate merger, and buyout acquisition process with international investments that included terrorism, this has cost American's money, and occasionally some people's lives. This expensive amount of money is tremendous with severe consequences, and sometimes will force the loss of some businesses. Upon this observation this even includes the American system of court proceedings with prosecutors that should recognize when these destructive crimes were committed as they have cost citizens dearly. Therefore this becomes an important issue of caution for them to take control of a business, or certain business assets, and even personal assets that America believes, and understands as valuable.

The nationality concern of most terrorist recently are Islamic radicals from the Middle East with enemy ambitions against Americans. These are some of the same people who are now becoming part of a growing amount of "nationalized Americans" who are sometimes small business proprietors. Another conflicting issue is that these business owners did not have to pay taxes for seven years. This non-tax paying equation has to be observed within the concept that them, and or others from mostly OPEC, and or Middle East countries have also caused, or supported damage that have cost American tax payers, and the government severely. Within understanding, this has occurred in most American states with values from the U.S. federal government whom has continued to give them this support to buy various businesses. Considering this, in the same process the diversion of businesses put a vast amount of American born citizens in a position where they can't even afford the purchase of a business. During better times in America more citizens could work and establish, or buy businesses, but less American people working, and various laws that need to be enforced has made this level of prosperity severely complex.

America being a well-developed nation consists of thousands of corporate businesses that are publicly owned, but the aspect here is that they depend on American workers that stimulate the U.S. economy.

The other side of the equation is a discretion of concern exist within foreigners making buyout acquisitions of American businesses like Inland Steel Company, Bethlehem Steel Corporation, LTV Steel Corporation, Zenith Corporation, and Amoco Oil Corporation. These issues have been part of critical American businesses being taken over by foreign businesses, or businesspeople that sometimes don't hold strong on various U.S. Constitutional values. Therefore the American people have loss another resource of business in which some of these companies also consisted of technology that foreign businesses, and people are working to improve.

The Zenith Corporation was taken over, and is now controlled by LG Electronics which is a company in the Republic governed region of South Korea. In South Korea, companies such a Hyundai, Samsung, and LG Electronics are businesses that are privately owned with hardly any competition similar to a communist state within strict rules. LG Electronics biggest foreign competitor is Mitsubishi of Japan which between these two businesses it would almost consist of war before any type of merger or buyout would ever occur. Understanding that most Asian businesses are "privately or government" owned, this even more so becomes a factual concern that applies to the U.S. Constitution, and U.S. National Security laws when they do business in America, and how they must comply with these laws.

Observing the difference between the U.S. and some foreign businesses that are owned by their government, America must be observant that certain foreign governments don't hire spy's to cause problems to U.S. businesses or citizens with involvement of business ownership. This is the factor that is sometimes indifferent from corporate investigations that may be parallel to government investigators for issues like the misuse of money, fatal accidents, or other conflicting problems. Anything less harmful than the 9-11 terrorist attacks in America against financial matters by people supporting foreign concerns (c/o Treason or Espionage) can have a possible cost to Americans that can be tremendous. This vital cost includes some citizens losing their productive opportunities of owning a business with logical expansion. Also this becomes the conditional value that when these terrorist attacked American "business and government facilities" including people, this became a severe coat to American taxpayers. Then American citizens have observed a long list of other crimes that should have been a concern. Financial crimes like insider trading, and anti-trust law violations are problems that they, and others would also get involved in to control certain financial matters. Therefore all foreign or new citizens with various business or government agendas are not always a good issue for America, especially if them or Americans ignore the Constitutional laws with violations against the establishment of Americans values.

International investment's, and terrorism are issues that the American society must be protective against when enemy countries will seek any type of harm. This includes from when the best of American government values, and the U.S. Constitution are not considered for the people, business, and government. The American money circulation has been hit hard when Americans recognize not only the $60 million dollar insider trading prosecution of Raja Rajaratnam, and two other men involved in Middle Eastern concerns, upon which they made illegal significant financial gains. These financial advancements deterred other American economic concerns from them acting unlawfully in business, but also various corporate buyouts are then part of major losses to Americans. This was another severe loss to the money circulation throughout the United States that keep lawful economic bookkeeping astute. Between domestic and international investment bankers, and the resource of public, and private businesses of America, a concept of this wealth has been shifted to various foreign countries causing a loss to American values of opportunity.

Understanding the international buyouts which included the American corporate acquisition of Inland Steel Company, LTV Steel Corporation, and Bethlehem Steel Corporation by Lakshmi Mittal a U.S. nationalized citizen who is originally from India has been part of a conflicting repercussion. In 2005 Mittal Steel spent $4.8 billion dollars on steel maker Kryvorizhstan from the Ukraine. Also in 2005 Lakshmi Mittal invested $9 billion dollars in India to build a Greenfield steel plant. We must hope that this leveragability of lending money is not similar to the $300 million dollars that was somewhat spent on a non-workable energy plant that GE Corp help build which the Enron Corp invested in with management duties in India. This Dabhol Power plant in India was too expensive for the people in India to operate which then the project was deemed as a "white elephant".

Observing these energy and steel industry concerns this format of corporate business led to Mittal Steel becoming the largest steel company in the world. This resulted from transactions during 2006 when Mittal Steel leveraged mostly U.S. corporate assets, and international assets to spend $32 billion dollars for the Arcelor steel company of Europe, and then changing their name to ArcelorMittal. Observing these factors with people of a Middle Eastern decent, and nationality from India, these issues provided billions if not a trillion dollars of investments to these Arab countries. Considering this, a vast amount of money that was spent in these Arabic speaking countries whom have terrorist roots with threats to the American society has allowed the loss of a percentage of one of its most vital industries (c/o steel) to an international conflict. Therefore even (c/o this time of war) sending enormous amounts of money outside of the United States into these Middle Eastern regions becomes an issue of national security, and a concern within the control of the global economic system.

This American money circulation (c/o being trillions of dollars combined), and issues of businesses on American soil continues to be vital to the prosperity of Americans. This is an issue that American and international investments are not paying off at a pace that is not fast enough for some Americans to economically recover from the previous recession. One of Americas strongest allies is London, England, (c/o the UK), but the BP corporate acquisition of Amoco Oil Corporation has been a large and complex transition of wealth from America. Understanding that international business issues occur from time to time various Americans can still be vulnerable to foreign business activities that defy the American laws, and or logical opportunities to prosper. This resource of billions, or trillions of dollars is tremendous with BP after the buyout of this American company which has had 2 severe accidents that were very expensive with damages. Considering American, and international issues of financial losses (c/o 2010) this concern for the economic progress of the American society is vital. Also this has crippled various business, and local government matters that may take longer than a decade to restructure from. Therefore it seems that a vast amount of corporate manufacturing or industry assets that earns Americans a wage, a pension, or investment interest with income from various products have been sold off to complex foreign governments, and business investment concerns.

Now the American money circulation in certain parts of the United States, and throughout the Mid-West of America have taken a beating. This is relevant with a certain amount of Americans not having money to invest, and diversified foreign businesses taking control of U.S. corporations, and even some small businesses. In the oil industry observing American gas stations with various Middle Eastern decent owners in certain parts of America, they have lately during the first decade of the 2000s been part of corporate franchise owners. This factual observation before certain issues got worse seems to look like a monopoly of totalitarianism. Upon this understanding they then changed the name of the corporate gas station's to become independent owner operators. Following these factors they eliminated a conditional amount of earnings to the well ran U.S. oil companies. Then also this outlines that they have no concern about providing truly productive investment dollars, or helping the earnings of profitable interest in those American corporations.

When these foreign people in business take control of American businesses, it usually consist of investment dollars between them and Americans which includes the overall value of income earnings, and U.S. Constitutional progress that has occasionally been ignored. These become losses to an expanding U.S. economy, and expanding businesses which is vital to the American soiled assets, people, and the future of the United States. This becomes the format of a well-managed economy with businesses expanding, and not being diluted from economic insecurity. Substantially this even includes commodities like oil that is obtained, and or purchased within drilling rights. This is a cost from various foreign countries, but also this is part of the importance of all resources in America maintaining their useful values of business without destructive interference.

Other conflicting factors are becoming a subject of how a vast amount of woman cannot hold manageable discipline of certain businesses, or corporations against men in America, and sometimes people from other countries. Contrary to this a few woman like Ursula Burns the CEO of Xerox Corporation, and Meg Whitman the CEO of Hewlett-Packard Company are businesses with good earnings, and important products making their jobs challenging. Some women do well with certain companies that provide products exclusively for woman, of these companies, and some others have been hit hard with illegal conflicts. Other concerns lately includes when some woman managers (c/o even CEO's) support mostly "woman or gay people concerns", and leave logical men out of productive business or government. This is a big negative problem for American men (especially in black American communities) that serve hard working disciplines, and occasional professional standards. Understanding this issue which includes more American woman working then men, this condition of logic has also included the contradictions of how some woman have been treated bad, and threatened like various woman in the Middle East. Actually the more foreign people that migrate to America, the more certain U.S. regions seem to be like other undeveloped countries like in certain parts of the Middle East, various "Third World" countries and places similar to even Africa.

Apart from violent crimes, more women in America with conflicting or ignorant men are being moved from their membership, or relationship values with the Christian faith and church. This has been factual to be a problem, and a loss of morals which is becoming a serious problem. This is even more so a problem with young people that are growing up to live with a bad attitude, and having illogical disciplines that don't consist of productive social, or professional values. This social condition of concern with not having a good attitude is guiding too many young Americans in a direction that eliminates professional, and occupational codes of conduct that is needed for America, and its businesses. Various standards within codes of conduct even from the words of Martin Luther King that were conditionally established within issues from the 1st Amendment resource of the U.S. Constitution are vitally applicable to the establishment of church, and a social standard of morals. Therefore these have become vitally important standards, and regulatory values for America, and the world.

Another value is the separation of church and state with Americans having a diversified Constitutional right to their religious choice, and this becomes an issue that should not be taken for granted. This becomes one of the values of weakness that American families within business ownership, and professional offices such as engineering, doctors of internal medicine, accounting, and banking are struggling to restructure from. Also this includes what is needed in all levels of productive businesses, and government to uphold these values in a responsible way without destructive conflict. Therefore this is vital within the understandable importance of how a family can support prosperous business ownership, and potential growth which has somewhat been a losing subject. Then this becomes some of the American business concerns that are consistent to the U.S. Constitution of how some city, and town governments exist.

The laws of church and state with its values of separation have suffered a downfall, but some have held their foundation to be helpful to the American people. This potential loss of the church is closely part of the establishment of family values, employment, education, and business ownership that has caused great harm when wrongful manipulation is applied. Throughout the decades of business in America this has included a certain amount or a majority of business growth with vitally important moral social conditions. Understanding these important values this format of relevant levels of experience came from people that consisted of family values, and logical stability throughout life that is "better known as Wisdom".

Observing how America has similar values with leadership to other developed countries with family businesses this has been recognized with Ford Motor Company, Hess Oil Corporation, Eli Lilly & Company, Johnson's Publishing Company, and a vast amount of others. Understanding the family business structure throughout America can be a vitally strong factor that logical people hold appropriate and respectfully. Then this is an important observation with decision making if a buyout or merger factor is considered. These are the moral values upon which the husband and wife of the household works to ensure that their children are well educated heirs to an estate, and the family business. The conflict of indifference was with the Block family of East Chicago, Indiana that established Inland Steel. Then observing Inland Steel took on a vast amount of investors similar to U.S. Steel with one of their founders being Albert H. Gary, the first mayor of Gary, Indiana, the indifference occurred when Inland Steel was sold to a family from India. After more than 70 years of business, and even community issues of involvement, it's conflicting that another resource of Americans could not buy or restructure this company which becomes helpful to American communities. This corporate merger then includes the concept of another group of people which are from the Middle East which is part of international business, but we must be observant about this investment, and any issues of potential terrorism. Therefore just like the people that attacked the U.S. on September 11, 2001, this included at least 30 to 40 other national security concerns that were a conflict to our tax dollars, national security, and hard work that may be at a critical disadvantage.

CHAPTER ELEVEN
LEGISLATURE, AND THE COURTS
WITH MERGERS, AND BUYOUTS

‖‖

Understanding the American system of government from local, county, state, and U.S. federal concerns including the concept of jurisdictions various corporate mergers, and buyouts have been pivotal with diversified issues within the American economy. This effect throughout the courts, and with important legislative concerns have offered the American society tremendous values of transitioning the U.S. economy as it applies conflicts mixed with capitalism. Observing these corporate and government conditional values of resource to most citizens close to certain businesses, and all the way up to the highest levels of the American system of government, these matters must be taken serious.

The buy or sale process of capitalism for acquisitions of a business has been an issue on occasions in the federal courts, and with observed concern by various state and federal lawmakers. This becomes the process that more American people must take future government concern of with various issues applied to a restructuring of a well-developed format of business, or the governed society we live. Some argumentative acquisition issues have consisted of the Paramount Pitchers Corporation VS Time Warner, Unocal Corporation VS Mesa Petroleum Company, and a few others with internal conditions of restructuring. Other good, and bad conflicts include the activities of those at AOL Inc., and more so telecommunication companies with arbitrary internet services. These arbitrary internet companies, and software companies like Netscape Communications (an AOL subsidiary), and Microsoft Corporation have been businesses that have been proposed to investors (c/o consumers) with new technology. These internet and communication companies (c/o some merger, buyout, and lawsuit issues) have been recognized for their arbitrary contributions to the U.S. economy during the first decade following the year 2000.

A vast amount of factors were understood with the arguments surrounding Unocal Corporation against Mesa Petroleum, upon which the smaller bidding company seems to take a loss with financial advancements. This also occurs over issues similar to non-agreeable terms with a subsidiary company or parent companies like with the many subsidiaries of Time Warner Inc., and Paramount Pitchers Corporation observing conflicting decisions. Understanding this, corporate insiders and outsiders occasionally have disagreements about the corporate buy or sale process within economic and financial evaluated transactions. These become vital decisions by the board of directors and various top management officials, and therefore then the courts may be part of a solution for all other diversified investors. Theoretically a level of advancements within these business matters, and other corporate businesses were part of factual disciplines when publicly traded corporations are an attractive business issue for other businesspeople, corporate raiders, and corporations.

These factors of businesses become a theoretical condition that must be repeated with advanced technological decisions for various older American companies, firms, and businesses. This format of business is different from new technology markets with other expanding business issues. As this applies to companies like Trans World Airlines (TWA), and their arguments within negotiations between corporate raiders Carl Icahn (c/o Icahn & Co), and Frank Lorenzo there was numerous issues observed with conflicting developments. This was a bidding war between 3 or 4 businesses and individuals to establish the way for control of TWA. Then considering this was part of an American asset transaction of equity to gain manageable control of this large airline company, this consist of a large, and important issue that the winning bidder would have to be committed from day one with long term goals that work.

Understanding various issues in the Airline industry throughout the United States Frank Lorenzo restructured Texas International Air (TIA), and created New York Air before making a hostile takeover of TWA. The TWA proposed acquisition by TIA was an aggressive move due to the fact that TIA was 20 times smaller than TWA, and their parent company Trans World Corporation. This lasted from 1992 up until 2001 which then consisted of American Airlines Corporation, the bankruptcy courts, and the U.S. Department of Justice. TWA Corp then after a 20 year struggle with bankruptcy, and labor union strikes, their consolidated resource of arguments, and diversified negotiations became the ownership concern of American Airlines Corporation. This level of ownership with U.S. and worldwide airline companies also consisted of issues such as National Security, and the U.S. Civil Aeronautics Board. Also with a vast amount of transactions the Securities and Exchange Commission had numerous duties to review these business transactions. This included their many fillings within a majority 10% holdings of corporate stock purchases. Therefore the procedures also have to be considered vital to keep the American society of business fair, and logical with these business transitions.

Although there are not many laws about how a person, family, business, or a corporation will agree to sale or buy a business, these values are conditionally part of the laws that exist surrounding this format of activity for a lawful resource of transactions. Two of the most aggressive corporate raiders within this process have been Carl Icahn, and T-Boone Pickens which lately during 2012 seems to be a dying breed of executives. Frank Lorenzo was another raider/entrepreneur upon whom during 1981 to 1990 was the CEO and Chairman of Continental Airlines upon which he was observed as the executive that took them into bankruptcy during 1983. Observing this process within resources of a discipline for transitioning the American economy from corporate mergers or buyouts can hold steady economic value if all lawful concerns are properly managed within the laws. More so hopefully they are laws that are good for American businesses, and the people with economic concerns for the future.

The Emergency Economic Stabilization Act of 2008 is the most recent legislature that has closely brought various corporate mergers, buyouts, and bankruptcies together with lawful, and or conflicting awareness. This format of legislature from the United States government moves to enact productive values of the Troubled Asset Relief Program (TARP) which carried some of the highest levels of Corporate Welfare in the history of the United States. This program and legislature was signed into law by President George W Bush, and during the Barack Obama Presidential administration the financial crisis has continued to be a bad problem. These same economic problems included other foreign ally countries (c/o Europe, Greece, Italy, and others) having economic hardships. This seemed like an endless problem even with the bailout of the U.S. Financial system, and with an enormous amount of people, and businesses throughout America, and the world suffering. They then even found themselves in a tremendous "Corporate Welfare" state of living which led to radical movements by crowds of people protesting. As this applies to businesses in America the format of corporate mergers, and some buyouts are now a severe duty of recommendations, and reviews by the individual states, certain courts, and more so the regulators of the federal government.

The concept of legislature applied within corporate mergers and buyouts occasionally exist when conflicting subjects occurred like U.S. Anti-Trust law violations that are discovered, or when insider trading conflicts are detected without good enforcement. This became vital within lawful regulation to keep asset liquidity guided throughout business. Another vital concern occurs when certain corporate management, and or corporate board members have disputes about future plans. Observing some speculated greenmail cash economic factors will more than likely be an issue especially when a corporate raider is involved, this becomes an investment accumulation of money. The combined concept of cash, and ownership values from holding large quantities of a corporations stock in a lawful capacity sometimes is a constructive challenge. These shares of corporate stock are held with buyout considerations that affect the liquidity of the corporation with most times a positive or negative repercussion. Therefore these liquidity factors of the corporation are a variation from some legislature, or court ordered matters that may become opinions of the corporate raiders, and or other shareholders.

Some issues of consideration in a corporate hostile takeover upon which some investors, and business executives consider are structured with argumentative negotiations, these agreements become similar to what the "Chairman of the Board" may consider for the company. This is considered important (c/o good or bad board decisions) when having conditional conflicts that almost seem similar to blackmail. Then with irrelevant business concerns this can be unlawfully harmful to business, government, and other American social values. Observing this process of negotiations the accumulation of greenmail cash is sometimes increasing with value for the corporate raider which very few laws can effect. These are issues which can be a violation of law observing "Obstruction of Justice", or be very helpful to keep the business operating in a normal, and resourceful way. Then these issues are sometimes lately not recognized good enough, and occasionally anti-trust laws have become closely observed with speculated obstruction of justice concerns for various economic, and social issues of greed. Observing these factors with various social conflicts have put a hold on smaller businesses from expanding with the American economy, and this affect has caused a vast amount of U.S. citizens to suffer job security.

Another effect on corporate merger, and or buyout business liquidity concerns comes with at least three major issues within U.S. Anti-Trust law regulated disciplines. The helpful laws in a government capacity for these business factors are the Sherman Anti-Trust Act (1890), the Clayton Anti-Trust Act (1914), and the Robinson-Patman Act which in 1936 was amended by the Clayton Act. When the Clayton Act was amended, this was done observing that it held value for diversified businesses throughout the United

States with anticompetitive law conditions. These are the laws that gave American small businesses a resource to operate against large corporate businesses. This is conditional to 90% of American (small or large) businesses having opportunities with logical, and fair business resource standards in America to achieve progress. Also this is somewhat a value of logic for corporations, and businesses to be lawfully competitive with fairness. The format of these competitive business issues should be pursued without the larger condition of business, or market control pushing other businesses out of a sectored market similar to an illegal monopoly.

Certain new industries have made business, and the people vulnerable in subjects of law that exist within the U.S. Constitution, and U.S. Anti-Trust laws that are conditional to damage if restraint is not applied in markets, and or business operating details. These fast maturing markets within internet, software, satellite, and computer companies have been some of the occasional business issues were the laws of anticompetitive practices have been vital with argumentative issues in some courts. Even more so the American telecommunications industry with wireless communication companies has created new markets. These new markets consist of diversified products that provide network programming from the internet, telephones, computers, and even television services. Therefore these services are providing information technology on the smallest, to largest electronic devices which have become a resource of strong marketable products with combined services.

Various other issues of legislative concerned resources included the repeal of the Glass Steagall Act during 1999 which sent banks, and financial institutions in numerous directions of economic conflict. The worse part of the decisions was to repeal of this "Lawful Act" established by U.S. Senator Carter Glass, and Congressman Henry Steagall which was a reliable source during the 1920s. Considering 90 years later the repeal of the Glass Steagall Act has been disastrous observing the fact that these men had an upfront evaluation of the depressed matters within sad economic conditions, and times in America. They had experienced these issues of the Great Depression and lived thru the suffering with observation of other people somewhat confused or nervous about banks and businesses during the stock market crash of 1929. Then considering both men having opposition as a Democrat, and a Republican awareness, them working together to solve the problem of how the banking system failed, was truly an important evaluation.

Following the 1929 stock market failure, and crash of the American financial system with the Glass Steagall Act, and the Securities & Exchange Act managed to consist of factors within economic security which held banking steady for over 60 years after those tragic times. This becomes a U.S. government process that allowed more increased value within overall business asset liquidity in their control of America's economic, and financial disciplines. Alan Greenspan was the Federal Reserve Chairman, and later after a decade in office he was criticized for some of these actions. His economic opinion before the worse part of the financial crisis consisted of when he pushed for self-regulation (c/o the Glass Steagall Act Repeal) in the financial sectors of banking. Therefore self-regulation, and deregulation was not appropriated with careful, or logical decisions.

The format of issues between self-regulating, and deregulating the laws lead to very complex industry, and banking problems. This was somewhat bad considering Alan Greenspan being an economist, but he failed to observe that the Enron Corporation and Kenneth Lay their CEO hired hundreds of investment bankers that don't understand engineering, and energy. He did this apart from being an energy based company needing professional, or knowledgeable engineers to help lawfully manage this business process if it was to be workable in the first place. These people at Enron being an "Energy Trading Company" was a severe failure, and this lingered into an over exaggerated banking industry. Therefore Alan Greenspan being a banking professional was also mislead by some of these other diversified economic issues of heavy industry in America. Theoretically this was not only his job, but others should have been alert also.

The legislative branch, and various businesses with corporate executives during the 1990s up to the year 2000 pushed for deregulation in various sectors of corporate business that offered conflict. Contrary to the additional problems in the telecommunication industry, and the American banking industry both groups within government and industry pushed for deregulation. Throughout this "bad" issue for excessive bank liquidity, and asset increases the legislature within the Glass Steagall Act provided an additional resource of format within a formal money circulation. This became an issue of too much "money", and too much "new technology" not to be regulated right, making this a critical point of the deregulatory conflicts.

New technology is a vital issue to observe within the need for proper regulation, and the use of technology surrounding the enforcement of the Glass Steagall Act which regulated banking. This also included values of commerce banking establishments being able to own investment banks which became a conflict to establish true values of equity. This was a severe problem I understood considering that the Glass Steagall Act, and the U.S. Constitution (c/o new technology like the internet) carried to much importance during the decades following the lessons of the Great Depression to repeal. The repeal by the U.S. Congress was a big mistake during the end of the Bill Clinton Presidential administration especially with Hillary Clinton being originally from the Chicago area with certain constituents in those financial banking district concerns. Therefore with additional technology to do things faster, and with more money being circulated in banks this became an advanced level of harm.

The Gramm-Leach-Bliley Act replaced the Glass Steagall Act upon which consisted of three congressional Republicans within Phil Gram, Jim Leach, and Thomas Bliley Jr. whom were somewhat working in a conflicting direction. This conflicting direction was for the possible good of the banking industry, and more so the bad of various people, and their equity within households. This also included economic problems which sometimes consisted of them providing bad managing disciplines to their business conditions to establish overall equity, and not hard earned liquidity. Just as no group of U.S. Democrat's, Republican's, or independent political constituents and, or professionals prevented the 9-11 Report Terrorist attacks, this included the "Debt and Mortgage crisis".

Both the 9-11 Report attacks, and the American Debt and Mortgage crisis is where we as Americans allowed complacent government, and business to harm the American society we live in. This gave more Americans economic, and social despair more than most times in U.S. history. These issues, and factors of harm affected most every large city in America with conditions of suffering that also included a vast amount of smaller cities, and towns that were already suffering financially. Therefore this deregulation process became a severe problem. Even more so this being a time of war, the American society surly has a duty to be careful with money, and issues of good, and bad foreign relations.

In the U.S. telecommunication industry (c/o the FCC) with deregulation, this has consisted of issues with internet companies similar to some rap music problems that ignore a format of indecency laws, and other concerns along the line of violating U.S. Anti-Trust laws. Also various telecommunication issues have lingered with people in corporate businesses or government with conflicts that occasionally become severe when obtaining information illegally caused destructive social activities. Some of these issues of conflict have destroyed small or large businesses in America while supporting an enemy foreign agenda.

Certain Americans, and myself have observed various subjects within the tremendously conflicting business activities that occurred from WorldCom Corp, AT&T Corp, and more so their truly sad subsidiary within Ameritech Corporation. This issue within observation of the FCC also was considered with conflicting corporate activities from Sprint Corporation, Nextel, and Verizon Communications Incorporated. Understanding the process, and or establishment of Verizon Communication which was a combination of the Bell Atlantic companies; they have held certain levels of business market strength over the last 10 to 15 years. Then with observation these business values of strength have existed throughout the decade of 2000 thru 2011 with conditions of a well-established majority of business operations.

These issues of regulation have been important with values over the decades leading up to the years of 2000, upon which government or even business competitors recognize the need for laws or more so the courts to intervene. This has even occurred with the AT&T Incorporated "proposed acquisition" of T-Mobil USA which is in conflict with Sprint-Nextel Corporation, but the U.S. government was the first to object to the $39 billion dollar merger/buyout with further judicial review. Observing the 1999 Sprint Corporation, and WorldCom Corporation's proposed merger priced at $129 billion dollars, this merger was not allowed by the U.S. government, and regulators in Europe due to anti-trust laws. An issue such as this within the "Sprint/WorldCom merger was a value within taking control of a market, but also not being able to provide long term nonpublic, or publicly held monopoly values in business. Theoretically between the nonpublic monopoly values of the American society this business process is not only the control of a market, but also a concern for high standards of liability, and managed liquidity.

Within these marketing factors the determination to control a vast amount of market issues within customers was obtained with a few other transactions including the Sprint-Nextel Corp merger which was then negotiated, and completed. This was a combined merger/buyout upon which these two companies created an expanded non-monopolized business to compete in a tremendous market in America, and considerably throughout the world. These government and corporate issues with some arguments on monopoly evaluated legal conflicts through a court hearing level of procedures is the observation that controlling a market can cause conflicting business harm. Then other hard working business issues can have fair market laws, and regulation on their side of prosperous business. This usually consist of a lawsuit from logical opposition, or a conflict from the government regulators with challengers that end up in court proceedings to "approve or disapprove" of the transaction.

The concept of deregulation in the telecommunication industry changed with some factors of technology that needed more research, and managing to be done property for the general public. A tremendously different problem occurred with deregulation in the United States financial markets has been an issue that has caused many factors of inadequate financial security, and harm. Between the U.S. telecommunication markets, and the U.S. financial markets most deregulatory problems have consisted of various issues for lazy or complacent reasons. These are issues that have been part of losses within responsible banks, and investment banks, for the logic of too much money lacking appropriate lending standards, and responsible standards in business that apply to U.S. Constitutional values of importance.

During the first decade of 2000 Fannie Mae, and Freddie Mac which are U.S. government sponsored enterprises where part of a troubled mortgage crisis. This increase of liquidity with hardly any additional business equity, and household equity in an unproductive mortgage lending market did not consist of enough professional planning. These disciplines within valued legislature, and appropriate business took normal citizens for a ride full of cash lending that they could not pay for as a legal commitment. Understanding this credit, and lending crisis with conflicting involvement between government, businesses, and consumers this conflict was observed with 26 million Americans unemployed, and 4.5 million families in foreclosure on their houses. Then the banking officials, and their institutions loss a large accumulation of assets as well at most times with numerous banking establishments applicable to their entire business. This was far from being productive after the repeal of the Glass Steagall Act with a mortgage, and business bankruptcy crisis becoming worse from 2002 to 2011.

Another issue that has been ignored or misconceived consisted of corporate mergers or buyout activity that destroys various conditions of tax revenue in America, and issues similar to U.S. National Security. A vast amount of these laws were established for the lawful, and sometimes rapid concept of unlawful activities that divert taxable revenue. Considering tax revenue is used by government for everything from defense, and national security, to highways, sewers, Social Security, and Welfare this is a money circulation of importance for government, and the overall society. Within this money circulation of tax revenue issues that were ignored, this conditionally hurts the U.S. financial markets, and various business matters as it applies to equity. Also local government, and some corporate or small business issues become prosperous within this format of a money circulation. These leveled percentages of budget valued cost for appropriated duties are valued with mostly responsible legislature, and other branches of government. Apart from the Great Depression days of the 1920s leading up to the years of 2000 various laws were ignored, and then the process of tax revenue has loss equity disciplines along with business losses.

Considering corporate or business acquisitions some legislature, and court intervention help's the regulatory discipline of large transactions of money, and business asset holdings. These asset holdings are sometimes massive with equations of economic corporate transitions that are vital conditions of buy, and sale responsibilities for the best format of executive decision making. With these issues of discipline the lawful control of logical business competitive resources is governed with a logical structure. Other laws have been established to keep some American technology from going into the hands of wrongful foreign enemies of America, and its allies. In 1975 U.S. President Gerald Ford created an executive order establishing the committee on Foreign Investment in the United States to delegate Presidential and government oversight on foreign companies buying U.S. companies. To some extent this is part of protecting American business assets which needed expandable levels of equity, and security for the overall American society.

Observing another concern includes how legislature has been established, but the concept of some legal court proceedings occasionally have been ignored, or misguided. This activity has negatively affected the legal, and Constitutional support that various small investors or business owners whom work to expand productively need. Their need of business law preparation is occasionally a legal fight in their market, business, or customer base, and usually considering this it consist of various social values to achieve domestic tranquility or ambitious concerns for prosperity. Although a new start up business is different with conservative values, a variation of large corporate businesses usually has a vast amount of "lawyers, or expert professionals or constituents". In a large business these people are on staff to keep, and maintain a lawful order in the business plan. These are resources of professionals to keep a business operation from being disrupted, or to prevent a business slowdown from occurring. This also includes losing a productive, and or well supported level of customer satisfaction. Even with productive business law professionals on hand in various small or large businesses during 2007 thru 2010 a vast amount of banks, and businesses still suffered, and were forced out business.

The format of banks, and investment banks were business operations in the U.S. financial crisis that during 2007, to 2010 had no hope to recover on their own. Not one troubled financial institution was able to restructure without extensive help from the U.S. federal government bailout plan. For example Ford Motor Company did restructure, and Bear Stearns investment banking company did not! This level of help from the U.S. government for mostly banks including some businesses, and a concentration of U.S. taxpaying individuals receiving stimulus checks was theoretically a provision of value through the TARP program. The only financial institutions that has come close to restructuring on their own has been Fannie Mae, and Freddie Mac whom are enterprises sponsored by the U.S. government. Considering this government support from TARP initiatives, the American society had suffered such a problem that most people as citizens, and a vast amount business owners did not have time or understanding on how to deal with the 2008 economic crisis.

One objective about the American system of state and federal government officials that work with the U.S. Department of Justice is do the lawyers know or respect the U.S. Constitutional laws? It has been slightly evident that a vast amount of lawyers leave a tremendous amount of reservation from their state government Bar Association oath to the American society, and the overall profession of law. After a tremendous amount of reservation, and political pandering a certain amount of law binding business owners including their constituents within occupations, and professions must struggle to eliminate any problems they may endure in the American society. Sometimes these have been new unspoken values of what seems to almost be communism. This has been part of the Endless Loop Crisis within factual conflicts that have put homeowners in the streets moving from location to location. Contrary to the streets this logic exist within how it has provided issues that have given them a loss of equity by forcing them to move into a different house, or apartment from their past ownership of a foreclosed house, or establishment. Also this includes excessively high propriety taxes, and even businesses being forced into bankruptcy which some of the same results have a reoccurring affect, and repercussion.

Upon understanding the transition that the American economy has endured a consistent format of law binding professionals with the individual state, and the U.S. federal Constitutional laws becomes the logic of all values to survive. It becomes complex to the understanding that the U.S. Constitution along with various individual state Constitutional laws could have prevented the banking crisis from 2008 to 2011. During 2008 26 banks closed; in 2009 there were 140 bank closers; in 2010 there were 157 bank closers, and in 2011 there were 88 bank closers. These are a major part, and tremendous concern of how government, and the people must restructure to have a vibrant economy. Contrary to these numbers, the FDIC also arranged a process upon which they recommended buyouts of most of these bank closing establishments. Therefore these values were established for another qualified banking establishment to buy them out. Then the FDIC supported the takeover, and the restructuring of all of the management. Considering this, then the restructuring of these bank/business assets for those American banking depositors involved with various banking companies had a relevant format of guidance. That's how the American society of people, and todays banking industry on occasion survives.

CHAPTER TWELEVE
BUSINESS COMPETITION, AND ACQUISITIONS VS THE U.S. ECONOMY

||||||||||||||||||||||||||||||||||||||||||||||||||||||||||||||||||

Observing the American society of business, and even the United States government's logic of industry competitive values, this resource of business acquisitions, and competition are vital issues that apply to the good, and bad of the U.S. economy. This becomes a factor that has adjustable concerns with the economy throughout the United States, and sometimes other countries which is a shared concern by many people in businesses, and government. Also this industry format and issue of competitive businesses with a conflicting economy has led the United States Postal Service (USPS) to consider many changes during the end of the 1st decade of 2000. These are changes due to the economic times in terms of how they have been a public monopoly sense the 1770s with Benjamin Franklin as the first Postmaster General. This observation with today's restructuring within America's changing times, and the economy consist of Patrick Donahoe as the Postmaster General.

Upon observation of the U.S. Postal Service during 2009 and 2010 their expanded business monopoly has taken on new challenges. Their conflict at the USPS within expanded issues are now being considered for change which consist of their many sorting facilities, and delivery concerns to scale back excessive cost and tax revenue losses. Various things like paying bills, or sending emails through the "internet and or telephone payment systems" as an applied service have reduced the amount of paper mail that requires a stamp which is one way that the U.S. Postal Service earns money. At the same time observing today they must stay competitive against companies like Federal Express Corporation (FedEx), and United Parcel Service Incorporate (UPS) upon whom are worldwide operating American businesses.

Contrary to other delivery business competitors these 2 companies (c/o FedEx & UPS) have historical values of being aggressive with lawful disciplines in mostly the package shipping industry. Observing the U.S. government operated postal service (USPS) most comparable competition consist of the same laws that apply, but business values are conditionally different from a government sponsored enterprise, and or a public or private monopoly. Considering their enormous resources, various business matters are sometimes geared towards the concept of employed people, and assets (c/o money, equipment, and facilities) being managed with good services to their millions of customers. Within the concept that labor unions were a factual involvement in all of these issues of business, the level of productive work, and efficiency was also a factor for various levels of business progress. This goes along the factual problem that some cities in the United States has consisted of too much labor, and not enough management minded people with their decisions to advance business ownership to create a better economy.

The conditional resource of the United States Postal Service, the Federal Express Corporation, and United Parcel Service Inc. consist of shipping and delivering millions of packages a day. This also includes the enormous amount of letters, and documents that are sent from one location to another which is based on industry and government standards such as within all Zip Codes. With the coordinated issue of corporate activities at the Federal Express Corporation with their CEO Fredrick Smith, and the acquisition of Caliber Systems Incorporated was a corporate merger acquisition that upgraded their business. Caliber Systems Inc was better known as Roadway Express, and or Yellow Roadway trucking corporation.

FedEx Corp adding Caliber Systems to their format of business was a conditional resource of logic to increase liquidity. This then consisted of additional truck shipping and property distribution values of advancement to become an even stronger competitor.

The package shipping business and industry has a strong concern within how they make additional progress considering FedEx Corporation was established in 1971, compared to UPS Incorporated being founded in 1907 with decades of formal changes. United Parcel Service has existed with a stronger customer base of sales, and has now continued their business disciplines during the 1st decade of 2000 as they are delivering about 6 to 9 million more packages then Federal Express Corporation. Contrary to the UPS Inc. buyout of Mail Boxes Etc. in 2001, other competitor's consisted of DHL, Canada Post, FCHL Worldwide, TNT Express, Royal Mail, Japan Post, and India Post. Also there has been others like LYNK Express (c/o New Zealand, UK) whom was also bought out by UPS Inc. in 2005. Therefore even with the Federal Express Corporation acquisition of Caliber Systems Inc., and them a trucking company has been an added positive resource. Then the FedEx Corporation's earnings, and asset values from this observation continues to outline that UPS Inc. is still the dominate monopoly.

The United States Postal Service delivers about 10 million less packages then United Parcel Service Inc. which means that there is a monopoly issue of competitive values. Understanding the U.S. Postal Service delivers about 10 million packages a day, and upon those managing a business process which has suffered with certain conflicts, this is part of their transition to restructure, or hold steady with the economy. With UPS Inc. having more than 450,000 employees during 2011 including their CEO Scott Davis, they have overcome most obstacles in the recent economic crisis. These obstacles even consisted of doing business near a war zone. Other challenges in America, and other parts of the world has become the increase in fuel cost, the European debt crisis, and doing business in other parts of the world were caution has become an important requirement. During the year 2011 UPS Inc. has more than 330,000 of its employees in the U.S. and 70,000 worldwide which provides a level of business progress that consist of helpful conditions worldwide, and more so the American economy. Contrary to these factors other relevant conditions of business liabilities exist including Constitutional laws (similar to U.S. Anti-Trust law values) which must be supportive or evaluated to keep the American economy productive with equality.

Another reason why United Parcel Service Inc. is such a productive U.S. company besides U.S. Anti-Trust laws that apply to monopoly businesses, they have a consistent discipline to also work with government regulators in a productive capacity. Having a large fleet of trucks, and even extensive airplanes like wide body Boeing, and Airbus distribution modeled aircrafts, they work constructively with the U.S. Department of Transportation (DOT), and the Federal Aviation Administration (FAA) keeping travel, cargo, and flight disciplines safe, and effective. As it applies to being a good corporate citizen they also work with the U.S. Department of Homeland Security (DHS), and the U.S. Department of Defense (DOD) conditionally as a contractor. Then UPS has also become part of a working group that stays in compliance with the Transportation Security Administration (TSA) to keep "national security" in order. Therefore with an enormous amount of government regulation these competing companies closely from time to time view anti-trust, and business law issues within the way they conduct business. Then this also applies to American values of discipline for the network of U.S. air traffic.

Observing the United States Postal Service during 2011 with their Postmaster General Patrick Donahoe the U.S. economy with a lower rate of tax revenue has forced the closing of hundreds of postal facilities. Also this restructuring and downsizing concept of plans consist of eliminating slightly more than 200,000 additional jobs out of their 574,000 employees during 2011. Besides their previous layoffs during the beginning of 1990 thru the 1st decade of 2000 these numbers are also similar to the closing, and loss of public schools, certain libraries, and then post offices. This has been the problem within crime that has eliminated young people which also has been tremendous in heavy populated black American cities.

Over the years before 2011 the U.S Postal Service at one time had slightly more than 750,000 employees, then following 1990 to 2000 enormous problems hit American cities hard with crime. Another issue of concern is that now out of 23,000 post offices 186 of those facilities have been closed, and various sorting centers are under consideration to be closed. As a competitor United Parcel Service Inc. has made profitable earnings exceeding $48 billion dollars during 2010. Also throughout their U.S. domestic and international markets including their business format of activities, UPS has made business investments in new properties to be effective in new markets.

Business competition in America has also routinely heated up between Ford Motor Company, General Motors Corporation, and this even includes the Chrysler Corporation whom seems to refuse to be left out. Most of these business issues with competitive values have similar problems throughout the American automobile industry. This was the observation that existed within the restructuring process of General Motors Corporation, and Chrysler Corporation after both businesses during 2009 filed for bankruptcy. Contrary to these large American automobile companies the global economy within automobile businesses are creating a "currency and money circulation" from U.S. automobile competitors. These competitors within the likes of Kia, Toyota, Hyundai, and others with the likes of Volkswagen have accumulated international business values. Observing Volkswagen being a German company in a country with somewhat high currency rates they are still competitors with a few others of concern within this equation that includes the European debt crisis. Understanding these vehicle manufacturing companies in America vs. Japan, Korea, and the logic of other low currency rate countries that are accumulating American currency (c/o the dollar) at record rates this is an ongoing conflict of competitive business.

Observing the American currency markets, and the global market for automobiles is part of an equation upon which various issues such as the price of gas has proven to be a tremendous challenge. These are economic differences like buying smaller foreign cars to save gas, but the American automobile companies are not far behind, or lost upon observing this subject. This conditional concern is partly harming the sales of American cars that burn more gas then some foreign vehicles considering the consumers that want to offset the cost of increasingly expensive gas prices which they may pay for or buy. These differences within domestic and international markets also consist of products, services, and occasional conditions to merge, or acquire other helpful businesses. Between General Motors Corporation, and Ford Motor Company vs. 5 or more foreign auto makers the issue of sales, and more so services are a condition that hold industry standards, and cost. Understanding standards in foreign countries other than the United States becomes a relevant conflict of increasing the American format of disciplines within products providing a money circulation. These values also consist of being part of a global money circulation throughout other countries with dependable products that are important for items that are sold at a worldwide capacity to businesses, and consumers.

The concept of business competitors is a diversified concern due to the fact that auto part markers like Federal-Mogul Corporation, and the Goodyear Tire & Rubber Company have held a strong American and international business presence. The Chairman of the Board at Federal-Mogul Corporation Carl Icahn is an active board member and company figure contrary to his "corporate raider activity" that has business awareness of their 45,000 employed people in 34 countries. The Goodyear Tire & Rubber Company has dealt with profitable earnings for years, but in 1986 had to fight off the cost of greenmail, and a buyout attempt by British businessman James Goldsmith. The James Goldsmith takeover attempt along with a group of investors from Hanson investments acquired 11.5% of the Goodyear Co. stock, which amounted to over 12.5 million shares of stock. The Goodyear Tire & Rubber Company then made a tender offer for their own company against James Goldsmith by purchasing more than 40 million shares of their own stock. This competitive retaliation cost the Goodyear Co. $224.6 million dollars, and appropriated a problem of forcing them to restructure their entire business. During 1990 to improve the restructuring at Goodyear Tire & Rubber Company they hired Stanley Gaunt whom lead them into a productive business again with their recent 2011 CEO Richard Kramer.

Considering two other former U.S. companies that are now owned by foreign businesses, Delco electronics, and Champion spark plugs have made this conflicting subject of competitiveness more favorable to foreign business. These businesses and corporations have strong levels of dependency on the 3 major U.S. automobile companies (c/o GM, Ford & Chrysler), and U.S. manufactures of motorboats, motorcycles, heavy machinery tractors, and other motor process conditions of machinery. Considering this the loss of American ownership within Delco, and Champion included their extensive amount of automobile products. This was critical due to being good American made products, and the valuable resources of these companies, and the American people whom prospered from them.

Federal-Mogul Corporation manufactures a vast of internal mechanical auto parts. These parts range from engine bearings, to piston rings, cylinder liners, transmission products, and other items that exist in, and or that are connected to most all automobile, and truck motors. Then Goodyear Tire & Rubber Company has made tires, and other rubber products for cars, and trucks that are distributed throughout America's auto industry with other distribution product values to locations throughout various parts of the world. Both of these businesses are publicly owned as American corporations, and with most auto parts, and or tire sales they have disciplines consisting of required safety, and quality standards. These valued products are vitally acceptable in all well developed countries throughout the world. Then both of these companies including repair shops with store fronts that sell parts are sometimes small privately owned "expandable" businesses. Therefore this is part of an enormous money circulation including the format of U.S. auto company dealerships in other countries.

Understanding the logic and competitiveness of various businesses is part of the people, investors, and the employees commitment to be prepared. This is valuable to any issues that include international economic values of currency, and product liabilities that the automobile industry may endure. In other countries they also usually have a tendency to carry supplies, or stock up on car and truck parts as inventory that are for the most common vehicles in a region or country. Considering this, these foreign and U.S. domestic auto part makers whom are competitors have increased their product accessories within automobile model details. This is also increasing the manufacturing, and sales of tires and various parts in the United States, and other countries. Therefore this is to competitively compensate services for the increased sales of U.S. cars, and trucks outside of America.

Business values on occasion becomes the concern of a foreign company's logic as a competitor against the U.S. domestic auto part markers of various car and truck models including name brand parts, and or tires to make an effect to keep a productive lead with certain products. Some logical examples are companies like Pirelli that were in competition for international race car events. Following this factor the main "corporate" tire vendors competing against BF Goodrich, and Bridgestone for this appropriate capacity within sales, and promotional opportunities on occasions still became Pirelli. This is slightly indifferent from how at the Indianapolis 500, and NASCAR racing events throughout America, Goodyear tires are the largest promoted tires, and are used in most of these racing levels of competition.

As it applies to normal street cars, and trucks these tires, and parts have specifications that are most all the time understood as having U.S. and some international safety regulatory conditions. This becomes relevant in America by government standards from the FAA, and DOT disciplines of legal roadway, and air travel tire, and brake system safety regulation. Then various countries with other lawful regulating values, and specified standards become the issue to buy the American or foreign products to appropriate the repair or replacement of parts on various vehicles. Just as government outlines these laws for business, and citizens they have a duty to keep roadways, bridges, and other infrastructures like sub-grade utilities in lawful order for the diversified activities of American citizens to be safe. Everything from stop lights, or stop signs to information or warning lights, and or signs are part of a circumference of lawful values. The jurisdictions of transportation, aviation, and waterways have local, state, and federal government levels of disciplines to work on together. This becomes the logic, and responsibility to solve any problems to this system or upgrade the infrastructure to higher workable standards.

The American concept of business standards with competitive conflicts can be recognized in the computer software, and hardware industries as businesses expand with various products, and or services. There are at least four American computer hardware manufacturing companies within Dell Incorporated, International Business Machine (IBM), Hewlett-Packard Company (hp), and Apple Incorporate whom are intense competitors in a market of technological discipline. These companies have an ambition to create new products, and earn logical revenue at rates that are in comparison to others throughout the world. Dell Incorporated is the youngest of these businesses that was established in the State of Texas in 1984. Michael Dell the founder, Chairman, and CEO along with 100,300 employees has lost ground to Hewlett-Packard Inc. in the personal computer (PC) market sense the year 2006. A certain level of success at Hewitt-Packard was established when Hewlett-Packard acquired Compaq Computer Corporation during 2001 and 2002. Following this buyout acquisition, the transaction has given Hewitt-Packard additional assets to take steps against Dell Computer Corporation's new found success in personal computer sales.

Dell Computer Incorporated had gross earnings of $73 million dollars their first year in business. During 1999 Dell Incorporated surpassed Compaq Computer Corporation as the largest personal computer manufacture in the United States. The valued issue within Hewlett-Packard paying $25 billion dollars for all assets at the Compaq Computer Corporation was an increase of factual business assets to take their desk top computer division, and even the laptop computer manufacturing and sales to a new level. Dell Incorporated making a good effort to compete with Hewlett-Packard is a devised indifference of Hewlett-Packard averaging income of $7 billion dollars annually to Dell's $2.5 billion dollars a year annually.

When a review is considered for the assets of these two companies that are owned by Hewlett-Packard it is part of their asset value of about $128 billion dollars compared to Dell Incorporation's $38 billion dollars in assets. This is the format within the time that Hewlett-Packard has spent in part with successful business ventures which has become logical evidence of good decision making in their corporate condition of management. Therefore Hewlett-Packard has held their market share in business as being a matured corporation in America.

The Hewlett-Packard (HP) company had other assets in their business that became part of certain productive spin-off companies such as Agilent Technologies in 1999 before the "HP" purchase of Compaq Computer Corporation. Agilent Technologies became a major business in the fields of biotechnology, electronic equipment manufacturing, and with logical distribution in California's Silicon Valley, and other parts of America. During the first decade of 2000 they have averaged 47,000 employees mostly between California, and Illinois that manufacture and sale scientific instruments, and semiconductors with over $7 billion dollars in assets. These issues of business at HP during the tenures of Meg Whitman, and Raymond Lane where extensive transactions just like a bidding war with Dell Computer Inc. to acquire the 3PAR company which they won with a tender offer of $33.00 dollars a share for the company. The 3PAR company is a "Data Storage, Server, and Software" company that became the HP 3PAR subsidiary of Hewlett-Packard.

Observing business activities between Apple Incorporated, and IBM Corporation an enormous amount of time has been spent on developing, and manufacturing computer products, and even communication devises that became important American products. The concept of Apple Inc. with Steve Jobs, and others took Apple Inc. computer into a competitive issue that exceeded the sales of certain products at Hewlett-Packard. Also these competitive issues at Apple Inc. has consisted of creating desktop computers, a popular set of laptop computers, and then the iPhone which has become a strong market of items throughout most telecommunication product markets. On the other hand IBM Corporation went from desk top computers, and mainframe severs that exceeded the level of networking computers that even Digital Equipment Corporation, and others could not easily compete with. Therefore these two companies including others have made business decisions that have gave them a level of progress that is productive in this highly competitive market for electronics, and computers.

Chapter Thirteen
Mergers, & Buyouts to Restructuring Business & Government

‖‖‖

The observation and challenge of restructuring a business, or any level of government during the first decade of 2000 has become a format of complex issues, and vital decisions. Considering the American economic crisis between the 1990s, and the first decade of 2000 to 2010 the logic within various issues has been slightly different from the Great Depression of the 1920s. One of the main factors that have hit local governments, and all other parts of the American system of government has been the loss of businesses with employees and their tax revenues to government. Observing the loss of government tax revenues this has caused government facilities such as libraries, post offices, and other establishments to close. This becomes the important logic within how large corporate businesses are helpful, but more so small expandable businesses, and how professional offices play a vital role within tax dollar revenue keeping government operational.

Understanding the variation of business in America we find the logic of understanding that small businesses can be part of a relevant, and productive society that helps government tax revenue. This is a working, and logical process that includes business expansion. These are small productive businesses that can make corrections within restructuring easier than what is needed occasionally in most large corporate businesses. This important factor is usually part of the determination of a business owner or the founder of companies like Dell Computer Inc., Microsoft Corp, and even Facebook Internet services. These are companies that have created a product, and or a service that people consider in demand, and their potential to make good profitable earnings becomes logical, and relevant.

The valued logic within prosperous times of the U.S. economy has made life in America somewhat most times good. Contrary to this factor, various corporations being a loss in society has given a vast amount of citizens a confused state of living, and this sometimes affects certain small businesses. Understanding this the U.S. economy had a few good years in the late 1990s which is part of this discretion. This vital concern consisted of an enormous amount of money being guided into conflicting directions between businesses, citizens, government, and even some supporters of terrorist. Also this included the condition of how American businesses, and the banking system throughout the United States accumulated suffering during the years following 2000, and especially during 2001. These issues were part of a group of diversified factors (c/o war time issues) that outlined certain corporations, and banks with some of their worse quarterly, and annual earnings within trying to make a profit. Upon this understanding a war time economy with other issues of business are part of good financial values, but are also part of the loss of life sacrifices with war, and vital government decisions.

Understanding this economy and various industries during the first decade of 2000 has been an issue with problems that America can label as occasionally complacent. These factual problems has consisted of issues within fraud, severe damages from explosions with fatalities in industrial plant operations, and a mortgage lending disaster with a credit crisis. Observing these critical problems include concerns of where banks have not easily found a solution to establish a logical recovery, or a process to be restructured to an effective level. An enormous amount of bankruptcies, and bank business matters are part of a concern that American citizens are suffering from within job security issues that keep them from making economic progress. This also includes various corporate businesses making an effort to recover from a loss of business, and banking progress. Upon understanding these factors just like the internet taking control of most news printed papers, the logical changes in the American society have given America challenges for the future.

Commerce banking institutions are lately during the first decade of 2000 buying out other failed banks, and they are becoming what is considered too big to fail if their economic conditions along with details throughout the U.S. economy don't improve. Citigroup, and Wells Fargo are two prime examples of banks that made decisions that pushed them into being a few of the largest, and strongest banks in America. One bank received the highest amount of TRAP funds (c/o Citigroup $45 billion), and Wells Fargo (receiving a smaller amount of $25 billion) whom bought out Wachovia bank. Following Wachovia being bought out by Wells Fargo they became the fourth largest bank in America. This is a rank and position that was once held by Wachovia, but now Wells Fargo has taken control of all of the Wachovia business assets. Wachovia failed without any hopes of restructuring besides being bought out, and this seems to be the normal "Point Of No Return" within the American banking industry. Therefore this circumference of issues within business, and government even as they bailout large corporations, and banking institutions still requires restructuring to a valid level of stability. Even apart from certain U.S. federal government funded support, this becomes the offering of these issues that require vital concerns, and good business management decisions.

Restructuring businesses during the 1970s to the late 1980s was a lot more rewarding and workable then business restructuring following 2005, and 2010. These where years when the U.S. Constitution seems to have a need to be more acceptable with observation by the American people, and severely by businesses, and even government. Then it becomes logical to observe a major example of business restructuring that consisted of General Electric Corporation, and a few others. Years later companies such as Apple Computer Inc., Hewlett-Packard Corp, Conoco (c/o ConocoPhillips) and the ups and downs of the American automobile, and airline industry where part of a bad economy trying to make positive ground, and economic discipline. Due to new, and some old technology the U.S. Constitution's 1st Amendment, the 4th Amendment and even the repeal of the Glass Steagall Act have made some people, and businesses hard to cope with for a prosperous future. Understanding this, the better format of government values that apply to business, and society consist of certain conditions of expanding with prosperity, and or domestic tranquility.

The General Electric Corporation restructuring (c/o the 1970s to the 1980s) was more so similar to that of the Conoco Inc. restructuring, but General Electric Corp was much more effective as of becoming a conglomerate. Observing that both companies go back decades within the concept of good, and bad issues of various U.S. economic times in America all businesses, and citizens involved had something to worry about. Within the logic of restructuring with various corporate mergers, and buyouts General Electric Corp (GE) became the factor of a prosperous business which included Jack Welch training, and managing large amounts of college students, and GE employees. Understanding this duty of training people that exist in most all businesses, this is a factor of guiding people, and then learning more to make the business go forward all together.

Contrary to students upon which a vast amount of them would become General Electric employees, there were other executive's managed by Jack Welch whom appropriated an increase in GE corporate assets, and more so revenue earnings. Robert Nardelli increased income at GE's power systems division appropriating economic values from $770 million dollars to $2.8 billion dollars. This was relevant due to a slowdown in 2006 of new construction which changed with an overbuilt real estate market, and mortgage crisis. Also he took GE's aircraft engine division from $7.8 billion to $10.8 billion dollars in 4 years. Jeff Immelt before becoming the next CEO of GE took the medical division from $3.9 billion dollars to $7.2 billion dollars in 5 years. The company's restructuring during the early 1980s through the late 1990s was tremendous with GE having increased revenues from $26 billion dollars to over $130 billion dollars. Their market value of General Electric Corporation went from $14 billion dollars to slightly above $410 billion dollars in 2004. Observing the vast majority of the company this was part of Jack Welch's ambitious talent within managing hundreds of corporate locations, and hundreds of thousands of employees. A conditional amount of these employees sometimes were moved around from one company to another by way of mergers in the U.S. and throughout a worldwide corporate capacity of concern.

Understanding Conoco Inc. compared to General Electric Corporation the format of business within both of these corporate operations is the fact that they survived the conflicting hard times of the Great Depression. Observing a vast amount of corporate businesses that also survived the Great Depression this was a financial loss to a vast amount of corporate businesses, investors, and American workers. Conoco Inc which was short for the Continental Oil Company expanded going along into the 1920s when they then merged the with Marland Oil Company. The founder, and oil exploration pioneer E.W. Marland, and his oil company which operated mostly between Oklahoma, and South Dakota as Marland Oil Company where part of various companies that suffered in the financial crisis of 1929. The Marland Oil Company with 600 gas stations in 1922, and with Continental Oil Company (Conoco) started having merger/restructuring discussions in 1928 right before the stock market crash of 1929.

Between the Continental Oil Company, and the Marland Oil Company a vast amount of business decisions were made within the effort of making these companies go forward. This included the Baltimore, Maryland refinery facility that Marland Oil Corporation purchased from the Prudential Oil Company which became part of Continental's existing Mid-Atlantic operation. Their Mid-Atlantic operation controlled 10% of the world production of oil during the 1920s and 1930s which included their regional operation within the marketing of these companies which became closely connected. The only level of oil production that can be compared to this level of supply within demand is that of Saudi Arabia, and their world production rates during 2006.

These companies that pursued mergers during the 1920s with the likes of the Marland Oil Company which was incorporated in Delaware had various revenue earning issues that needed vital improvements. This problem became the concern within the oil industry, other industry concerns, and the financial markets that were to provide productive values for investors, government tax revenue, and various resources for the American society. Following certain issues their business concerns consisted of millions of shares of stock which became part of a transaction of discipline for future considerations of business purchases, and planning. This also consisted of the Marland Oil Company whom became the purchasing company of more than 3 oil businesses, and corporations operating with duties of restructuring. Therefore they became part of complex mergers, and then appropriated a logical level of simplicity with the establishment of becoming one larger company with one name.

The format of mergers within restructuring (c/o June 1929) consisted of the Continental Oil Company, the Marland Oil Company, the Prudential Oil Company, and other lesser known commodity production stock listed company affiliates. Contrary to competitors like Standard Oil Company these economic, and financial values consisted of a certain amount of additional affiliate companies listed on the stock exchange whom agreed to be one company that could make them more competitive. This newly established company going into the 1930s was named Conoco Incorporated which was the most well-known business name with logical economic earnings. Now from their 2002 merger, Conoco Inc. became part of a restructuring process upon which the company's new name became ConocoPhillips Company with their merger of Phillips 66 (c/o Phillips Petroleum Company) which was to improve their competitive position even more in the oil industry. This merger made them the 2nd largest oil refining company in the United States, and the fourth largest non-government controlled crude oil refinery in the world.

When corporations, and small businesses seem to merge in their conditional business directions these are usually corporate issues that consisted of the times within America were jobs are loss or they are restrained until economic times improve. This is especially true for U.S. government projects which during the first decade of 2000 various infrastructure engineering, and construction projects became a vital need. Contrary to this fact an enormous amount of government facilities within places such as libraries are being closed which becomes a loss of vital resources to various cities, and towns. Also the United States Postal Service is making reductions in staff, and evaluating the closing of various facilitated locations that cause a severe complication to citizens that depend on these government services, and assets.

The equation between management, and labor union issues have become a part of this concern during 2010 which is a problem for a well governed town, city, or regional society. Chrysler Corporation, American Airlines Inc., United Airlines Corp and LTV Corporation are a few conditional examples. These conflicting issues consisted of management providing offers of incentives, and labor unions that would not accept hardly anything to help, or work with LTV during their bankruptcy. Then later LTV and other steel companies became foreign owned businesses. Both Chrysler Corporation, and American Airline Inc. spent the last decade with extensive labor negotiations that sometimes slowed down productive business, but it was vital that they work together. Even after United Airlines loss tremendously after the 9-11 Report terrorist attacks months later they were threatened with a labor union strike. Considering these factors became a problem that the American society of people within business, and government have made decisions on; some activity was illegal, or had become an anti-American business issue. This is part of the American society we live in to recognize corrections, or important negotiations in a timely format of resources. Then the citizens, which includes clients of these businesses (c/o even banking) with concerns were left even more so with restructuring government, businesses, and social values. These contingent liability conflicts, and unlawful levels of confusion will need to reestablish their societal values, which will take at least a decade or more to fully be recovered.

The concept of a government equation to restructure labor union concerns lately during 2011 includes the State of Wisconsin's Governor Scott Walker's actions of making an effort to eliminate collective bargaining from the state union workers in Wisconsin. Considering this state and federal government observation the U.S. Postal workers, and librarians are usually workers that suffer less injuries than most other labor union oriented jobs. This is a labor union, and educated business issue of format within low level observation. Then the consideration of these factors means that they should be able to manage the cost for long term details in a low volume cost facility similar to a library.

The collective bargaining issue is a factual concern, and observation that some labor organizations should take under consideration the equation of economic values of business or government to exist. These are labor union conflicts that make it difficult for them to exist for all other employees. This is a level of existence whether in government or various businesses upon which both management, and labor have a need to survive or exist productively. Therefore keeping business operating cost low, or logical should have been a factual challenge, and achievement for some business owners, and or executives which includes government officials. Then these operating expense duties (c/o tax dollar spending) to exist with logical advancements of stability are factual within their overall concern of liabilities.

Governor Scott Walker of the State of Wisconsin outraged an enormous amount of citizens that support any factors of labor unions, but Wisconsin and other states with local governments are closing facilities, and reducing staff. When this happens the local, or regional citizens, and even businesses have less money in a budget to appropriate services that apply to additional jobs. This observation includes them being deprived of services, or they are denied the support of important things such as the upgrading of certain parts of the infrastructure. Some localities have went as far as to eliminating or reducing fire departments, and police department positions (c/o even collective bargaining) whom also have labor union values of concern that are part of government tax revenue values.

We must remember that police, and fire department officials including citizens use the same good, or dangerously bad roadways. A vast amount of these roadways may need repairs before a disaster occurs which is a vital concern. Understanding these two issues within labor unions, and the infrastructure a resource of officials within Scott Walker, and other officials in government or a business management capacity must make careful decisions that are critical to labor union activities. Then the labor unions have a responsibility "not to be" destructive with decisions, economic evaluations, and or provide a commitment of logical work duties, and discipline.

These become the factors of how the American society of government, and businesses must have just as much "management" as there are labor union members, and concerned resources between these parties. This is a process that helps create levels of progress for businesses to be established, and expand with the economy. An objective of vital importance is that anyone with an understanding of managing can leave government employment or a business after earning logical income within money, and start a business. A small business that expands is helpful to the business owners, and society including the levels of improvements that should not be put in jeopardy with unlawful conflicts.

A better format of business means people becoming engineers, construction contractors, bankers, teachers or internal medicine professionals which includes them establishing themselves as business owners or maintaining a professional office. This becomes a Constitutionally vital part of a well-developed American society. Then overall with other businesses this also becomes a vital part of governments progress with taxation which applies to the "laws" and " tax revenue". These are revenue values upon which most government officials, and assets then can be managed with a logical money circulation. Understanding this also becomes an appropriate and helpful part of social values for the citizens, and their standards of living. Therefore this is the format of values that will increase the level of managing taxable revenue, tax dollar spending, and the duties that are productive for the American people, and a governed society to prosper. Then economic, and financial domestic tranquility apart from government can be achieved.

Becoming a Right-To-Work state observing the geographical concerns of individual state governments may not be the complete answer for restructuring local or state economic concerns, and various financial issues of vital importance. Some conditions of labor unions, and the diversion within Right-To-Work conditional laws can sometimes be a bit unfair or rational when heavy labor union concerns consist of health benefits, and financial security values. Also this unfair, or complicated balance of working can be part of the compatible issues to strenuous levels of work duties. The observation here most times require special, or vital benefits that keep a workers ability to perform at productive rates considerably good. This becomes the reasons why the U.S. Department of Labor consist of regulated laws within the Labor and Management Relations Act, and the Taft-Hartly Act that where established with labor union issues in mind. There are less than 24 Right-To-Work state government regions in America during 2011, but more importantly a conditional amount of these conflicting states consist of illegal immigration concerns. Observing this a threshold of lawful government, and business values are then established.

As a vast amount of illegal immigration problems mostly occurred in Right-To-Work states that are mostly "in or near" southern states like Arizona, Texas, Florida, and Nevada these states have suffered different international conflicts between other U.S. regions. Contrary to New York with 9-11 these places have become conflicting regions that have accumulated problems that moved into other northern states along with illegal immigration. Some of these state government concerns also have issues with some people that have supported terrorist that hate America, and this becomes similar to the illegal drug trade from Mexico. This was done to the extent that they have gotten involved in the financing, and planning of various acts of terror against America. Therefore the "American" labor union support, and the diversified issue of paying all employees consist of an occasional bad mixture of problems that government along with business must keep in legal order. These are then benefits, and economic values for employees, and their families that have been guided into the hand of enemies of America whether this is from various regions of the world, the Middle East, or even some U.S. neighboring concerns of Mexico.

Observing the need to restructure a vast amount of local American governments during the 1st, and 2nd decade following the year of 2000 will consist of small, and large businesses including government working together. This becomes the managing process of where economic growth at all levels between the applicable disciplines of government, and business will become vital. During 2012 two American industries are starting to make additional progress, and be helpful within a return to America's economic level of prosperity that is important. Those two industries are the automotive industry with General Motors Corporation, and the agriculture industry with businesses like the Kellogg Company which is connected to the other productive operations of business, and industry concerns like farming. There are other markets, businesses, and industry conditions of value, but these are business issues with interesting conditions for restructuring a business, or even an industry that requires legislature. Therefore with an arrangement of sales, employment, and product disciplines their business expansion, and restructuring values have been occasionally helpful to America.

General Motors has been a corporation that has restructured its self with many changes. Their 2011 CEO Dan Akerson has made decisions to freeze the salaries of 26,000 of its U.S. employees until certain goals are achieved. General Motors Corporation also has achieved some levels of restructuring, but within their commitment to an enormous amount of retired auto workers, and executives their pension fund accounts with management duties are under-funded at about $8.5 billion dollars as of September 2012. These are commitments that occasionally are restructured by the company that they pay out with other benefits such as health insurance that are vitally important to retired, and active employees. Contrary to Detroit, Michigan and the automobile industry which has international economic repercussions; throughout the State of Michigan they also have the Kellogg Company as a major food producing company in Battle Creek, Michigan. Kellogg Company is somewhat surrounded by the Mid-West agriculture commodities within Indiana, Illinois, Ohio, and even Iowa where soy beans, wheat, corn, and other vital commodities are important to their business. These are commodities with conditional by-products that appropriate a resourceful money circulation throughout the industries of farming, and agriculture.

The Kellogg Company has operated for over 100 years starting with their founders Will K. Kellogg, and John H. Kellogg creating various food brands that mostly where geared towards breakfast meals. The Kellogg Company with their last two chief executive officers David Mackay, and John Bryant over the last two decades before 2010 has been a company that buys other food companies or product divisions that will benefit their company. This is done when other valuable companies need restructuring to survive, and or it becomes valuable for a company like Kellogg to expand. Then these levels of expansion became important within the values of the Kellogg Company, and its operating discipline of increasing their products to consumers, and their income earnings. They also have increased their business product divisions to include other food sectors like snacks (c/o potato chips & crackers), and a few frozen packaged food items, and products.

As a worldwide company Kellogg International consist of business in 23 different countries including their activity and headquarters in the United States. This becomes the logic that American companies will do business internationally, and buy foreign businesses, which may include property. These become valuable decisions for various future business activity with logical concerns, and within making purchases these business decisions may consist of what they consider a good price, or investment. Observing this factor they have purchased various food brand business divisions from certain companies like Diamond Foods Inc., Procter & Gamble (a consumer products & personal care business), and an array of carefully chosen foreign food businesses. These are businesses between Asia, Germany, Russia, Australia, and the United States which includes some other developing countries.

Understanding newly developing countries with the observation of corporate America concerns over the last 10 to 15 years (c/o 2012) this has become a new part of business restructuring. A logical example has been observed within how General Electric Corporation has created light bulb manufacturing plants in Indonesia. Another observation is how Ford Motor Company, and Delco have opened plants in Mexico which now includes Whirlpool Corporation during 2011, and 2012 with the manufacturing of washers, dryers, and refrigerators. These are measures upon which these companies save money in labor cost, and therefore they can offset a level of high operating expenses, and still sale products at a rate that is acceptable to American values of weak or strong currency ratings on various products.

The American small, large, or corporate business atmosphere is still a logical resource for expanding or restructuring businesses besides heavy involvement in other low currency countries. Considering these values of business survival this becomes the format of managing business to keep economic values workable. This becomes valid whether a business is just starting from scarce, or is bought into the format of new owners or management. Upon this observation an enormous amount of businesses could not restructure upon which they ended up liquidating all of their inventory, equipment, and or properties to close out retail stores, distribution centers, and or manufacturing facilities.

Liquidating, and bankruptcy issues in America during, and before the 1st decade of the millennium year of 2000 has had a tremendous effect on the U.S. economy. This becomes the fact of businesses such as major department stores, and their regional business offices which more than likely have gone out of business, closed, and liquidated a coordinated amount of assets. The concept of liquidating as many assets as possible including inventory to pay certain issues of debt is mostly a court ordered concern, and level of procedures. Montgomery Ward's, Service Merchandise, Marshall Fields & Company, and Circuit City Stores Inc. are a few big name retailers that are part of this observation. Then this becomes the tremendous factor of how some business values within patriotic customers found themselves in a mood in which they loss a good dependable place to shop.

Montgomery Ward's was more so one of the most tremendous retail corporate businesses that was established in 1872 that folded after bankruptcy, and liquidation during 2001. The company slightly came out of bankruptcy proceedings, and protection between 1997 to 1999, but they depended too much on a major investor within GE Capital which is a subsidiary of the General Electric Corporation. Then with heavy economic losses during the next Christmas shopping season they announced their plans to close the business, and liquidate their inventory, and assets from at least 500 stores. Therefore this company that was well over 100 years old loss the discipline to operate as a productive corporate retail store business. Contrary to these factors they like some other corporate retail businesses had an "Endless Loop" concern that was similar to America's declarations to various war time issues.

Various issues to correct certain problems was factual considering the vast amount of retail store chains that went out of business. This was occasionally due to some regional, and even foreign business, and social conflicts. Some of these issues became so severe that it was enough with reasons for the United States government to declare war twice during a 10 year span against various regions of terrorist in the Middle East. Contrary to the 2 attacks on the New York World Trade Center these people within a terrorist capacity would also violate laws against smaller issues within American business. This factor of violations included U.S. Anti-Trust laws in the oil, and gas markets within service stations. Also affecting people, and business was the conflict of an enormous amount of illegal immigration problems with the U.S. / Mexico borders being terrorized by an illegal drug trade with similar conditions to war that spread into others parts of America. Considering this, various conditions of crime and war became a severe deterrent from normal business in America.

Montgomery Ward's contrary to them not being a U.S. defense contractor donated large quantities of consumer electronic products to U.S. Desert Strom troops in 1990, and 1991 which was part of a mistake. This level of generosity is valuable, but totally unexcitable in business. Observing this level of severe ignorance by the Montgomery Ward's business establishment is factored as one the worse business decisions in American history. This was a nice, and supportive thing, but a disastrous issues to their long term economic stability, and not a good business decision that anybody with common sense should have allowed. Upon these factors of business, this takes the highest level of management decision making for the best business results possible, and that did not happen in a long term capacity.

Following the first Persian Gulf war (c/o 1992) business problems lingered such as the lack of manageable effort within Montgomery Ward's to restructure their business which caused them to close around 500 store locations, and layoff 37,000 American employees. The repercussion was severe due to the fact that Montgomery Ward's had store locations in every state in America which especially includes most major cities, and various towns. This became one of the largest retail bankruptcy liquidations in U.S. history observing the year 2001. Their CEO Roger Goddu, and other top management officials were criticized for their poor performance which included the standard termination of the companies $1.1 billion dollar Employee Pension Plan for their retired workers. Therefore between the U.S. government, and Montgomery Ward's the company had to reevaluate the terms of commitment to an estimated 30,000 "Ward's" retirees, 22,000 active employees with retirement accounts, and the pension premiums to the Pension Benefit Guarantee Corporation.

Observing the Pension Benefit Guarantee Corporation (PBGC), and its duties as a U.S. government agency they guarantee participants over the age of 65 years old a maximum of $54,000.00 a year. This became effective as of the year 2011. Understanding companies like Montgomery Ward's, Circuit City Inc, and a few others that could not restructure, this agency now within the PBGC became obligated to hundreds of companies, and hundreds of thousands of retirees who's company pension funds failed.

During the year of 2010 the number of defaulted companies hit 147 who's pension funded plans failed, and this caused an increase in the PBGC's budget deficit to $23 billion dollars. This is a factual concern that means the American system of government is spending more money than their tax revenue income is when these corporate businesses fail. Nevertheless this means hundreds of thousands of retirees by law are being supported by the Employee Retirement Income Security Act of 1974 (ERISA) which is Social Security. Now these, and other retired people are being supported as participants of the PBGC which is usually a lower cost within benefits. Understanding this tax revenue loss the repercussion has an equation that put more pressure on the surviving corporate benefit issues that fair tremendously different. Therefore some businesses are a loss, and other businesses that consist of the best conditions of a corporate retirement plan like those at a vast amount of the more successful corporate businesses in America becomes a weaker resource within business, employment, and commitments to retired people.

The loss of four corporate retail businesses with thousands of stores, and employees all over the United States has left economic problems for most levels of government, the people, and various real estate markets in America. Understanding the real estate issues at Montgomery Ward's was tremendous, and this could have been the thought of being too big to fail, but that was wrong! Montgomery Ward's with the thought of restructuring a market (c/o more than 500 store locations) was a capacity of real estate, and a conflicting economy that meant the concept of restructuring would be complex, and expensive for the American society. This is part of the changing hands of ownership within real estate which becomes a very detailed process by local governments, and others in hundreds or more locations throughout America. Considering these factors this is the process of when large corporations are involved in a concern of conditional economic and financial issues of failure, bankruptcy, and then liquidation.

Observing restructuring attempts, and trademark issues, the business within Circuit City Inc. had a special format of architecture trademark values applied to most of their store front facilities. This became a registered trademark conflict within other businesses with investment concerns. These are conflicting details with transitional concerns that don't apply to other corporate business trademark values which other corporate businesses had to consider unworkable. This is a factor that provides additional complex conditions within their liquidation, and bankruptcy issue within procedures. These are a few of the conditional values upon which especially apply if another corporation is to consider certain merger or buyout investment issues that saves or restructures a business. Then this means the purchase of all existing business assets to be restructured is part of a logical business agenda. This is similar to Macy's Department stores Inc. moving into the Marshall Field's store locations (c/o Chicago) without a real bad trademark conflict after the buyout.

These defaulted business factors have left an enormous amount of properties in an already complex real estate market where foreclosures have been rapid. The American market within real estate has consisted of an enormous amount of changes over the decades, and century which includes affordability concerns, banking, and even the infrastructure. Upon this concern the economic, and business restructuring within real estate in most American cities, and towns has lately (c/o 2000 to 2012) consisted of a challenge for long-term stability. This becomes the indifference within today's U.S. economy discovering that $11 trillion dollars of household wealth had vanished (c/o 2007 & 2008) which became an issue compared to what occurred during the Great Depression with some conflicts that faired similar.

Circuit City Inc had over 550 store locations throughout the United States which means employees, and real estate properties had to be restructured by mostly government. This is also due to the fact that they could not find a corporate raider, or another corporation to buyout the company during their troubled economic times. These levels of business speculation becomes dangerous, and must be considered with corporate assets, employees, budget concerns, and future business planning values. Therefore with a bad economy and no merger/buyout restructuring this cost was handed out to the American taxpaying people by the American system of government.

As American businesses such as Circuit City went through these conflicting times for business, and even the consolidation of retail stores most issues concerning government could have done more. Some issues would have involved the courts, and Constitutional law concerns when certain Americans supported an enemy foreign agenda before the 2001 variations of war, but other issues were vital throughout the credit markets for buying goods, and services. Circuit City Inc., Marshall Fields & Company, and other retail stores like Service Merchandise were some of the first companies hit by the American debt crisis, and a few other conflicts. The American society within people buying cars, and houses is similar to buying televisions, stereos, and major appliances like they sold at Circuit City, and Service Merchandise. These are items that have a long term repercussion of being a necessity and holding economic values, but as people in America's credit borrowing network of banking went bad along with other conflicts these businesses like others suffered.

These are factors within the American system of capitalism that have been part of good, and bad conditions of logic. This is to evaluate a workable, and or a non-workable business environment which becomes part of important factors. The importance of this industry environment may require businesspeople involved with government making the right corrections. Even understanding the business environment at Marshall Fields & Company whom were bought by Federated Department stores this was not likable by a vast amount of their committed customers. Federated is the parent company that changed Marshall Fields & Company Chicago flagship store (c/o other locations) to become Macy's department stores with logical conflicts to become workable. This was a combined merger/buyout which most products, services, and employees had a vast amount of similarities. Upon these workable components in business the logic of the American society with business, and even government will continuously be changing, and hopefully with values of better stability, prosperity, and domestic tranquility.

CHAPTER FOURTEEN
AMERICA'S TIMES OF DIRECTION FROM MERGERS, ACQUISITIONS, & BUYOUTS

Throughout the American society a vast amount of corporate mergers, acquisitions, and buyouts have given people, business, and government an array of directions to evaluate future concerns that will effect everyday life. Some of these guided issues, and concerns apply to the disciplines within issues of tax revenues, logical business ownership, and productive employment with good conditions of expansion. Over the last four decades leading up to the year of 2011 the United States, and an array of state governments have consisted of various good, and bad issues of economic values throughout conditional industry concerns. This has become the business expansion resource that has changed the American society dramatically, and the fact that other future changes will be vital with good decision making.

United States Steel Corporation, Ford Motor Company, Kellogg Company, General Electric Corporation, and a vast amount other corporations have changed, and challenged the format of becoming diversified in business similar to a conglomerate. Contrary to a productive conglomerate value of business conditions this is not for all businesses, and therefore a business or corporation must maintain their logical direction within products, and or services.

This occasionally becomes the logic of why some companies last for over 100 years. Considering this these companies make the best decisions when they evaluate certain mergers, acquisitions, or buyouts which become part of the changing times that includes various government, and more so business assets which can be beneficial or workable.

Understanding the value of how various American companies, and businesses manufacture products, this on occasions has become more competitive with foreign interest which decreases the value of American currency. American currency provides logical tax revenue for government, and various resources for the people whom are making the best decisions in business, but most all people still must challenge inflation. Most times lately this includes foreign business conflicts, and or other concerns. These are business values that also include innovative issues, and ideas that give Americans the awareness that manufacturing disciplines must be evaluated for cost, safety, and quality.

Observing the 1990s, and the years of 2000 robotics, and technological systems for information, and computer processes have kept a vast amount of corporate, and manufacturing environments of American business productive. Contrary to these levels of innovation the United States must continue or improve their knowledgeable awareness of how various economic, and technology issues can violate the U.S. Constitution against citizens, and push America backwards. Therefore this becomes the format, and logic that various businesses, and even certain levels of government have managed to exist by in the American society with business for well over 100 years when you observe the best corporations of America.

The format of misguided economics, and production that exist in various businesses consist of matters that have somewhat been tremendously harmful to an enormous amount of Americans, and businesses. This becomes the resource concern of American citizens that could have survived, or done better if the best guidance within government, and business had occurred over the last 2 decades. These years before, and after 2000 with the first Persian Gulf war, and now with the Iraq, and Afghanistan war time issues have consisted of too many conflicting economic transitions. Understanding these transitional concerns have negatively affected a vast amount of industries, and people throughout the United States this applies to the future prosperity, and domestic tranquility of American citizens. Even American military veterans and personnel of foreign wars need jobs which are managed by Americans they can trust on American soil which may even apply to vital laws, or legislature.

Observing harmful conflicts by foreign competition, and occasional defamation of character by, and against Americans that instigated confusion this has left the U.S. with a financial crisis during the first decade of 2000 that will take years to correct upon who survives. This financial crisis also includes issues with an over built real estate market which is now part of a necessity of painful restructuring. These become factors of instability that can destroy a well-developed society. This is an issue of concern within a vast amount of subjects in an enormous amount of American regions that are evaluated between issues of a secured infrastructure, business survival, and a format of reducing crime. Then stability and advancement can be achieved throughout a well-developed, and governed society if most of these details can be improved.

The concept of U.S. government sponsored enterprises such as Fannie Mae, and their former CEO Daniel Mudd, and Freddie Mac with their former CEO Richard Syron became subdued in negative business concerns during 2006 thru 2008 with a foreclosure crisis that will take time for a good economic recovery. Considering this mortgage backed securities crisis the timing, and disastrous conflicts with these two CEO positions consisted of issues within duties that where not very likable in a leadership role. They both Daniel Mudd, and Richard Syron unlike Franklin Raines (c/o Fannie Mae) were removed during this economic crisis for poor performance.

Franklin Raines was one of the last of two CEO's whom had a bit of comfort with this job (c/o investigations) at Fannie Mae, upon which now them, and various other people and issues have become very complex. Even the turnover rate of CEO's at Fannie Mae, and Freddie Mac has become intense with some staying for 9 months to a year. This level of complex business also included additional government regulation which has made this one of the most extensive times in America to help the U.S. economy. Following the crisis within Fannie Mae, and Freddie Mac the vast amount of banks, and businesses filing bankruptcy, and going out of business means that America will conditionally take decades to regain various levels of business prosperity.

The economic crisis during the first decade of 2000 also includes the American mortgage market that suffered severely. This was a problem upon which millions of Americans were left in disarray causing some of the strongest banks, and companies that survived to move in the direction of buying other businesses if they are workable. Observing these conflicts Henry Paulson the former U.S. Department of Treasury Secretary evaluated these losses to be in the 10s of billions of dollars. This consideration upon which Fannie Mae, and Freddie Mac were in the forefront of being considered somewhat insolvent is a problem of long-term business decisions. Understanding this professional, and government concern within a resource of GSE's the U.S. government, and them did not have to question the concern of a bailout for these agencies, which was mandatory to correct within time. From 2007 thru 2010 a bailout type of restructuring of Fannie Mae, and Freddie Mac by the U.S. government had become an ongoing process between the administration, and legislators for the right government procedures. Therefore now even 5 years later this level of restructuring is still an ongoing process for government lending for commerce bank mortgages, and providing government secured investments within "Mortgage Backed Securities".

Observing the U.S. financial and economic crisis of the first decade of 2000 consisted of the American society of households losing some $11 trillion dollars of logical wealth, and then other tremendous problems could not easily be avoided. Also more than 4 million people "not only" loss their homes to foreclosure, an estimated 4.5 million American's loss their retirements, and their life savings during this crisis. With complex losses to people, the U.S. real estate market also has consisted of new commercial, and residential properties that could not be sold fast enough for a profitable price. Considering these issues of economic, and financial concerns, the direction of America has accumulated very complex times concerning the future years, and decades ahead.

The Federal Deposit Insurance Corporation (FDIC) has been part of government pouring out money to the extent of guaranteeing deposits, and taking over troubled banks throughout the United States at record rates during the first decade of 2000. The 411 commerce banks starting in 2008 to 2010 in America that failed, and closed during the Chairwoman Sheila Bair's tenure at the FDIC was a challenge for the insured deposits that bank clients are guaranteed. The insured liability of bank deposits guaranteed was amended from $100,000.00 to now $250,000.00 during 2009, which is a repetitious process that applies to the economy, and inflation over a variation of years. These are some of the important details within the changing times in America sense the Great Depression that has given America additional levels of economic security.

Even more so the conflicting economic times of 2000 has caused a challenge of theoretical evaluations for the U.S. government whom had to appropriate legislature, and this forced them to evaluate legal cases to understand the existence of this financial crisis. A vast amount of informative testimonial legal evidence, and information was obtained by the 10 member Financial Crisis Inquiry Commission. Their work consisted of the testimony of 700 witnesses during 19 days of public hearings between New York, Washington D.C., and other communities. These procedures became important with the establishment of the Housing and Economic Recovery Act of 2008 during the end of President George Bush's tenure. This commission created by the U.S. federal government received a vast amount of the vitally important details from testimonies about the American "financial and mortgage crisis". The understanding that they received was that this was necessary for the American system of government, and people to review.

The review from the Financial Crisis Inquire Commission (FCIC) during 2009 to 2010 included issues about deregulation, and the repeal of the Glass Seagull Act which the Federal Reserve Bank and the FDIC are still concerned about during 2012 with a very complex economy. The FCIC's conclusion consisted of the concern that there are commerce banks whom hold to mush unsecured cash (c/o liquidity disciplines) that may fail. Then this is the factor of where too big to fail institutions may occur. Therefore a failure would mean more deposits of money belonging to the people, and or as clients will have to seek restitution from the U.S. government, and the FDIC if an appropriate acquisition of the bank is not applied. Observing this concern, certain legislature became a logical necessity in this format of a "destructive money circulation" eliminating, and or causing problems to a balanced U.S. government budget. Therefore some issues of deregulation have been part of this problem without expanded liquidity which was not accomplished with manageable business disciplines by a certain amount of banks, and others.

Within various businesses that have been around for nearly a century the issue of how they operate within the changing times determines how they will survive. This becomes the observation of various issues of economic values with conflict, and the complex times applicable to the American economy. Today during 2011 Eastman Kodak Company, Whirlpool Corporation, Chrysler Corporation, and even some of the largest to smaller banks in America are suffering tremendous concerns. Over the last 20 years after Eastman Kodak bought out Sterling Drugs, and upgraded an extensive chemical division at the film company, a percentage of the company went in a direction that could not hold air in a corporate merger/buyout bubble. Their CEO at Kodak's film company Antonio Perez has worked in various directions such as with the marketing effort to sell a vast amount of their patents to create liquidity apart from bankruptcy. These Kodak patent issues exist for certain products, and various business divisions which also includes an online photo imaging business. This level of survival with Kodak's financial condition consist of the stock price selling at $1.14 a share which is a record low during 2011. The Eastman Chemical Company is a much more productive business with liquidity that has achieved conditional growth, and market value with the stock in 2011 selling for over $35.00 dollars a share.

The activities within Whirlpool Corporation have been another conflicting business venture that has left American citizens, employees of the Whirlpool Corporation, and government observant with concern. Whirlpool Corporation with their CEO Jeff Fretting during 2010, and 2011 consist of 70,000 other employees, but this American company is now sending more manufacturing jobs to Mexico for inexpensive labor. Their activity had been more extensive than a vast amount of other corporate businesses. Considering Whirlpool's corporate headquarters in Michigan, and the buyout of companies like Maytag, Jen-Air, Amana, Admiral, Hoover, and others they are eliminating factories in Iowa, Arkansas, Illinois, Tennessee, Mississippi, and Indiana. Even with this high level of restructuring throughout the United States Whirlpool Corporation has various rearrangements in Mexico. Also they are building factories and creating a vast amount of jobs which include conditional rearrangements in Canada that means this issue becomes part of their restructuring process to become a stronger global business.

Considering the direction of Chrysler Corporation along with the American automobile industry, an enormous amount of conflicts has occurred with divesture. With 2 out of the 3 major U.S. automakers filing for bankruptcy, and seeking U.S. government TARP bailout funds their future is still in question. During the year of 2007 and 2008 Chrysler Corporation closed hundreds of dealerships that consist of questionable earnings. Before this problem occurred, all 3 major American automobile companies where businesses that were slightly hurt financially in 2000. Then months later, more economic distress occurred after the September 11, 2001 terrorist attacks due to dangerous travel concerns.

Following these conflicting times within a credit lending crisis which became the next severe problem, and more so with other economic and financial conflicts on the rise, some American values of economic progress became questionable. Then later in the following years the Ford Motor Company's restructuring consisted of paying about 70,000 employees with a buyout package not to return to the Ford Motor Company. This was the companies decision for them to appropriate that certain employees take an early retirement from the company which became their format of business survival. Considering this the U.S. auto industry is at least a decade away from the levels of prosperity that they had in business years ago before this economic, and financial crisis occurred. A better direction for the company became the issue that they could accomplish prosperous earnings with good products, only "if business, and our governed society goes in the right direction" with stability that can be maintained.

The restructuring of the U.S. auto industry applies to the economic disciplines that the people, businesses, and government can comfortably buy cars, and trucks. This level of support within these businesses is critical for various social concerns that are helpful within tax revenue issues for government. These values also include the rates of production with vehicle sales that have become a tremendous concern. General Motors Corporation has slipped in vehicle sales observing them selling 5,017,150 vehicles in 1999, and 10 years later in 2009 they sold 2,084,492 cars and trucks which has been a continuous format of losses. The Ford Motor Company in 1999 sold 4,163,369 vehicles (c/o 539,660 the year following the 9-11 attacks) and during 2009 Ford Motor Company sold 1,620,888 cars and trucks. Chrysler Corporation in 1999 sold 2,638,561 vehicles, and in 2009 they sold 931,402 vehicles. Ironically Chrysler sold 1,085,211 vehicles in 2010 after their 2009 bankruptcy, and liquidation process while closing 789 automobile dealerships throughout the United States which was clear evidence of an economic crisis. This also more than likely included closing a few dealerships internationally.

Some factors from the Barack Obama presidency within the U.S. Department of Transportation, and the Environment Protection Agency have been part a government of lobbied law making process to eliminate carbon dioxide emissions from gas burning vehicles. This has become an issue that all vehicles on American roads had to consist of changes. These changes would consist of the help and lawful commitment of the automobile company's observing that this problem can be controlled with legislative disciplines. Contrary to the diversified issues within people, and the environment this would require that the future manufacturing of cars, and trucks would conditionally have new requirements that consisted of drastic mechanical changes. Also a big requirement by the automobile companies is retooling their manufacturing facilities. With these factors, and evaluated concerns the future issues of electric cars including the "oil and more so gas" industry has taken up various business loss precautions. These conditional precaution values with this technology change that could affect their industries product sales in the near future is a vital factor of planning.

These ideas from the American system of government, and industry will effect business throughout America in various ways. Even the format of an expansion for wind farms that include energy production wind turbine towers, the conversion of a business atmosphere to sale energy for cars is not a small challenge. This becomes the challenge of providing more electricity values within most people's homes. Upon this fact more electricity is needed when people have to plug up their car (c/o more than one automobile) every time they come home to keep car batteries charged. During these inflationary years of 2012 with gas prices at $4.00 per gallon have caused the American society to be part of a disciplinary, or discretionary economic movement. Upon these factors it's almost the same argument between wired communication vs. wireless communication, nuclear energy vs. coal powered energy plants, and more so gas motors vs. electric motor vehicles which becomes a big technological issue with complex investment values.

Observing some of these corporate businesses (c/o the automobile industry) they are rarely involved in corporate mergers, and or buyout acquisitions. This becomes a concern more than various critical business decisions, but their businesses are a vital part of the U.S. economy. A vast amount of other business contractors that do business with the automobile industry are an issue from time to time observing their conditional contract requirements, and business values of discipline. Then these business, and industry concerns apart from critical issues within banking consist of their core products within business. These industry concerns are the manufacturing of product materials like steel, aluminum, rubber, glass, and textile products. Observing these products, they are a dependable material resource for automobiles, and other large priced items that require financing from a bank. Also this includes the manufacturing of trucks, airplanes, ships, railroad trains, and their continuous or valued level of production. This is a vital economic, and budget concern for mostly the U.S. society within a large capacity resource of manufacturing. Also this becomes the understanding that various commodities, and their cost issues can affect various industry values. This therefore is a part of managing cost, pricing, and earnings which are a vital day by day duty.

The concept of coal mining in the United States has constantly taken tremendous hits with fatal accidents, and this is part of an occasional slowdown in production. There have been 2 coal mining accidents within 5 years of each other that should tell the American society that we are going full speed backwards in various industries. The Sago Coal Mine disaster in Upshur County, West Virginia which on June 2, 2006 killed 12 coal miners with 1 miner surviving. Another severe accident occurred on April 5, 2010 at the Upper Big Branch Mine in Raleigh County, West Virginia, and this disaster killed 29 coal miners with 2 miners surviving. This has been a severely bad half a decade considering 30 years ago 38 coal miners died at the Finely Coal Company in Hyden, Kentucky. Observing the problem that this occurred during 1970 before industry, and coal mining safety was included in "health, and safety" issues, these laws intensified considerably. This becomes an issue for management that may put them in a position to be rated as a junk bond for restructuring.

The United States Department of Labor officials with the Mine Safety and Health Administration (MSHA) was created in 1970 to regulate the mining industry to eliminate fatal accidents, and other mining related health concerns. As it applies to coal the MSHA Act and the U.S. Department of Energy where established in 1977 which was a time when industry and labor unions were fighting for better work conditions throughout America. Another factor consisted of the enormous amount of coal that was increasingly being used in the steel industry, and at coal fired energy utility plants. Therefore upon complacent conflicting issues during the 1990s thru 2011 the offices of MSHA, OHSA, and other government agencies allowed industry to become weaker due to a lack of occupational, professional, and or logical government involvement. This part of America was getting worse within maintaining various safe and productive work place environments. Upon these factors this especially includes industrial processes with heavy equipment operations, and various hazardous materials that have most always consisted of careful work details.

The direction of heavy industry in America with various business franchises have seem to come together for more foreign business owners in various U.S. regions other than American past, and future potential business owners. These become some of the U.S. Constitutional concerns within an Endless Loop crisis which more than likely caused a vast amount of diversified harm. This issue of a crisis included conflicting conditions within U.S. Anti-Trust laws, Constitutional laws, and various safety law violations that have gone unenforced, and or ignored.

Unenforced U.S. Anti-Trust laws has become a problem that has gave certain discretionary business owners a resource of illegal monopolies. These small business monopolies have come together for various foreign people which has left a certain amount of American's with a questionable future. The most observant conflict is that a vast amount of U.S. citizens as small existing or potential business owners have been put in a near too last place position making business ownership extremely complex. Then the placement of this provision vitally consist of new citizens from other countries having opportunities that outpace long term American citizen business owners tremendously.

Comparing these issues of foreign businesspeople gaining control within business ownership values it's important to recognize that even "fatal manufacturing, and industrial accidents" have increased tremendously which is a vital indicator that American safety standards have weakened. This has been conditionally observant in the oil, chemical, steel, and coal mining industries which has created various bad values within the concept of business, and even government excepting losses as well. Government will file law suits, and become aggressive, but lately when they get involved, people have been killed, and extensive cost is evident. Even various

American steel industry products, or industries where concrete is vital with various engineering and construction disciplines or sectors of business, certain government infrastructure upgrades where not considered effectively.

The professional concern of safety standards within conflict went along the format of manufacturing, engineering, and government evaluated procedures of various work having a need of vital improvements. This concern of issues to maintain waterway levee walls were not inspected, and did not hold up to save people, and their assets in various regions. Observing this was critical, especially when this problem included the 2005 New Orleans hurricane, and flooding disaster. This was the factor of rainwater and the accumulations of unregulated surface water that moved onto land from the Gulf of Mexico which destroyed an enormous amount of assets, and people. These also where important public safety regulation concerns that government, and professional engineers ignored, and now the tax payers have to pay the cost. Upon this observation these government, and industry values consist of harmful effects to the American society which is losing vital standards of discipline including social, and economic stability.

The National Oceanic and Atmospheric Administration (NOAA), and the National Aeronautics and Space Administration (NASA) are important to the U.S. government administrative concerns that apply to scientific studies, and various technical evaluations. These evaluations with logical, and lawful studies are helpful to understanding the environment, nature, and human survival in America when they (c/o NOAA & the National Weather Service) provide early warning systems about destructive weather. These entities managed by the United States federal government have been considered for budget cuts, and or a new format of research level of issues within technical goals. Also these 2 entities of the U.S. federal government have a vast amount of sub-contractors, and they provide an enormous amount of technical equipment that they use with their scientific projects, and studies.

The observation within 2 examples of how America makes progress with agencies such as at NASA, and the NOAA can be understood within hazardous weather, and issues of alert against terrorism. These are values observed within the conditional example of Hurricane Katrina, and the use of unmanned drones by the U.S. military during deadly missions. For one these are activities that have given citizens a warning that saves lives, and this gives them appropriate time to board up houses, and businesses within the protection of their property. The second is how the U.S. government eliminates terrorist network leaders that are dangerous to America. Some of these issues must not be taken for granted, and this becomes an issue were losses occur. Therefore the format of technology, and the commitment within government, and engineering responsibilities to help, and manage even the city of New Orleans consisted of severe problems. This was factual from the hurricane Katrina disaster were technology was workable, but upgrades to the infrastructure failed. The factor of this level of concern means a lack of personal, professional, and government disciplines were not applied, and then America was given a large loss.

Observing the extensive budgets at NASA, and NOAA their multi-billion agency activities have come a long way with inflation, and they have advanced with conditions of technology. Upon the understanding of how NASA economic, and technology advancements has helped an enormous amount of products was through various space projects. These were technology values developed in the United States with its logical condition to start with how certain details within NASA's Apollo rocket system worked with accuracy, and needed improvements.

The NASA space shuttle program today takes off from the launching pad, and then is carried into outer space by jet propulsion rocket boosters, and now lands on an airport runway like most all airplanes. This process is much different than the 1970s when a space capsule would splashdown ending the space mission in the middle of the ocean. This was part of American aviation advancements that were achieved. Satellite technology has also achieved advancements with the progress of developing 1000s of orbital satellites which have been sent into outer-space by various crews of astronauts on a spacecraft. Therefore business, and corporations that are regulated by the Federal Communication Commission, and the Federal Aviation Administration have been able to work together in coordination. This level of coordination has been relevant to give citizens logical conditions of new technology devises, and "sometimes" safer services.

The concept of new American, and or internationally made devises are a cross reference within different levels of products. These products such as cell phones with service agreements, and robotic processes of machinery especially like in the automotive industry have given America certain values of advancements. These and other products like jet engines, the brake systems for cars, planes, and other transportation products where part of these advanced levels of research and development at NASA, and NOAA. All 50 states in America, and throughout the world benefit from the National Oceanic and Atmospheric Administration when it comes to studies for lakes, rivers, and oceanic atmospheric conditions. The NOAA benefits are conditionally valuable within the activity of hot and cold temperature values of study, and volatile weather condition evaluations.

Between NASA, and NOAA these agencies have also created technology that helps small, and large boats and shipping technology. Upon these concerned subjects within navigation, underwater sonar equipment, and other technology that provides information concerning volatile weather, or sea life specimen conditions these products within certain operating systems have been helpful. This also includes predictions which are scientific values that gives America another resource within the concept of being a well-developed and lawfully informed society.

These procurements in most U.S. government fiscal year economic disciplines of conditional budget evaluations hold values that are relative for agencies of government business to achieve operational goals. NOAA is a scientific agency within the United States Department of Commerce, and they have operated with a budget during 2009 to 2011 which was appropriated at about $4.5 billion dollars to $5.6 billion dollars. The duties of NOAA are to help our governed society to be informed with the values, and uses of a comprehensive understanding of nature's activity within the oceans, everglades, coastal areas, and to live and work within these conditions of the atmosphere. Also NOAA consist of the responsibility to understanding the atmosphere with predictions of deadly or destructive snow with sub-zero weather with a blizzard, or high temperature weather even as they apply to tornados, or hurricanes. Then this also applies to changes in the Earth's environment, and to conserve a vast amount of marine water conditional resources to meet our nation's economic, social, and environmental needs. Therefore with these values the American society corresponds to various detailed activities. These are issues focusing on ecosystems, climate, weather, and commerce which includes transportation that is a coordinated discipline from the National Weather Service with extended radio, and communication resources.

Observing these diversified factors and issues that also are sometimes found in business mergers, buyouts, and extensive transactions, the American society including business still must have good corporate and business citizenship values. This becomes the value within American businesses that earn a profit, and then they can help various logical, and lawful causes that keep a vast amount of communities guided in a positive direction. Understanding this during the years of 2012, and 2013 the U.S. Constitutional values of wording that have been amended, and established as laws over their 235 years of existence are still a guide for the freedom of economic transitions. Therefore the logical judgment of every American citizen, business, and level of jurisdictional government must make their best effort to stand on established principals, and values to keep our American conditions of social, business, and government disciplines lawfully working together.

Index

Carty, Donald 30
Case, Steve 10
CBS 105
Cerberus Capital Management 53, 108
Champion 175
Chandler, Coby 46
Chapter 11 53, 66
Charlotte, North Carolina 28, 118
Chase Bank Company 2
Chicago 62, 80, 91, 138, 162, 196
China ix, x, 63, 85, 88, 94, 115, 142
Christian 152
Christi, Chris xvii
Chrysler 2, 52, 53, 54, 67, 93, 99, 103, 108, 115, 175, 186, 204, 205
Chrysler Corporation 2, 53, 54, 93, 103, 115, 173, 186, 203, 204, 205
Chrysler Financial 52
Chrysler Group LLP 53
Circuit City 192, 194, 195, 196, 197
Circuit City Inc 197
Circuit City Stores Inc 192
Citgo Corp 42
Cities Services Company 11
Citigroup 19, 20, 48, 49, 52, 112, 120, 121, 122, 123, 129, 182
Civil Defense 56
Clayton & Dubilier 28
Cleveland, Ohio 100
Clinton, Bill 7, 31, 33, 73, 144, 162
Clinton, Hillary 88
CNN 69
Coast Guard 60, 105
Colombia 115
Coltec Industries 28

Columbia Broadcasting Corporation 105
Columbia City, Indiana 84
Columbia Savings & Loan 5
Comcast 17, 66
Communication Act 26
Compaq Computer Corporation 37, 177, 178
CompuServe 65
ConAgra Foods Incorporated 40
Conoco Inc 43, 126, 183, 184, 185
ConocoPhillips vii, xii, 43, 44, 88, 89, 125, 182, 185
Constitution v, ix, xi, 15, 43, 55, 57, 67, 71, 76, 81, 82, 85, 88, 90, 103, 123, 131, 146, 148, 149, 153, 160, 162, 168, 182, 183, 199
Constitutional xiii, xiv, xv, 2, 7, 33, 34, 57, 58, 63, 70, 86, 92, 114, 123, 143, 148, 149, 151, 153, 165, 166, 167, 168, 172, 197, 208
Continental Airlines xii, xvi, 125, 157
Continental Oil Company 184, 185
Countrywide 49, 50, 112, 117, 129, 130
Countrywide Financial 129
Cox, Chris vi, 74
Credit Default Swaps 117
CSX Corporation 2
Cuba 88

D

Dabhol Power 150
Daimler-Benz AG 53
DaimlerChrysler AG 53
DaimlerChrysler Motors Co 53
Daly, William 91, 92, 134, 138
Davis, Gray xvii

122, 123, 129, 130, 131, 182
Westcorp 119
Western Union Company 41
Westinghouse Corp 105
Westinghouse Electric Corp 25
Whirlpool xiii, 18, 77, 78, 192, 203, 204
Whitman, Meg 152, 178
Willemstad, Robert 115
Williams-Striger 14
Williams Technology Group Inc 65
Wilson, Karen F. 92
Wilson, Woodrow 86
Workman Compensation 86
WorldCom vii, xi, 6, 10, 21, 22, 23, 64, 65, 66, 67, 69, 73, 74, 77, 128, 133, 135, 136, 138, 163, 164
World Savings Bank 119
World Trade Center 31, 74, 75, 193
World War I 106
World War II 62, 106, 141, 146

Wyeth Company 94

X

Xerox Corporation 152

Y

Yahoo 136
Yellow Roadway 170

Z

Zenith Corp vii, viii, 14, 55, 56, 57, 77, 86, 87, 99, 102, 103, 131, 145, 148
Zenon Environmental Systems 17
Zuckerberg, Mark 44

About The Author

▌▌

JAYSON REEVES was born in Gary, Indiana and is now an author whom writes on the important subjects of government and business throughout the United States of America. Jayson's writing is based on the experience that he has established within working professionally throughout design, engineering, and as an investor including businessowner. As an investor, businessowner, and former partner of a civil engineering firm he has observed, and experienced the American society throughout Indiana, Illinois, Arizona, and other states. This experience with valued interest includes the work, and observation of small, large, public, pivate businesses, and corporations with their adjacent values to government. These business disciplines within society, and with most values of government have become the foundation of his writing to enlighten the American general public.